Need-to-Know Spanish Verbs

lingualism

© 2022 by Matthew Aldrich

The author's moral rights have been asserted.
All rights reserved. No part of this document may be reproduced or transmitted in any form or by any means, electronic, mechanical, photocopying, recording, or otherwise, without prior written permission of the publisher.

ISBN: 978-1-949650-73-0

Written by Matthew Aldrich
Edited by Oscar Guzman and Matthew Aldrich

website: www.lingualism.com
email: contact@lingualism.com

Table of Contents

Introduction		ii
How to Use This Book		ii
Audio		iv
abrir	open	1
acabar	finish	3
ayudar	help	5
buscar	search	7
caer	fall	9
cambiar	change	11
comenzar	begin	13
conocer	know	15
conseguir	obtain	17
creer	believe	19
dar	give	21
deber	should	23
decir	say	25
empezar	begin	27
encontrar	find	29
entender	understand	31
escribir	write	33
escuchar	listen	35
esperar	hope	37
estar	be	39
estudiar	study	41
ganar	win	43
gustar	please, like	45
haber	have	47
hablar	speak	49
hacer	do, make	51
ir	go	53
jugar	play	55
leer	read	57
llegar	arrive	59
mirar	look	61
morir	die	63
necesitar	need	65
pagar	pay	67
pensar	think	69
poder	be able to	71
poner	put	73
preguntar	ask	75
querer	want; love	77
recibir	receive	79
saber	know	81
salir	go out	83
ser	be	85
tener	have	87
tomar	take	89
trabajar	work	91
venir	come	93
ver	see	95
vivir	live	97
volver	return	99
Answer Key		101

Introduction

Spanish conjugation tables can be quite dry and boring, but they don't have to be!

Need-to-Know Spanish Verbs presents them in a fun and colorful way, using a layout inspired by mind maps. With these 'mind map' tables, you can see at a glance all the different ways to conjugate a verb in Spanish. They're easy to follow and understand, and they'll help you memorize the conjugations more quickly and efficiently.

Inside, you'll find tables for the fifty most common, essential verbs used in Spanish today. Each table is followed by a guide to the verb's meaning and usage and also exercises to help you master the conjugations and use them correctly in context. Both the conjugation tables and the exercises appear on the **free accompanying audio tracks**.

The exercises are aimed at elementary and intermediate learners who have some previous knowledge of Spanish grammar and how to use various verb tenses. But even beginning learners will find the tables and accompanying audio useful to gain a solid foundation in Spanish by memorizing common verb forms needed in everyday communication.

How to Use This Book

Need-to-Know Spanish Verbs is essentially two books in one. First, it is a reference showing the conjugated forms of verbs, their definitions, and their usage. Additionally, it is an exercise book for improving your skills in Spanish and expanding your knowledge.

You can approach the materials in a way that best suits your learning style, needs, and level. For example, you may choose first to study a table (while listening to its audio track and repeating what you hear) and then tackle the exercises immediately or the next day (to test your long-term retention). Or you may wish to try the exercises without first looking at the tables to test yourself and see how much you actually know already. You could then refer back to the table on the previous page to double-check conjugated forms before confirming the correct form in the answer key at the back of the book.

The Tables

The tables are divided into four gray boxes with labels for the three moods (indicative, subjunctive, imperative) and participles. Inside the gray boxes are color-coded sub-categories (tense, etc.). The conjugated forms for each tense are arranged in the traditional layout for conjugation tables–two columns with three rows. The left column is singular, while the right column is plural. The first row is first person (I, we), the second is second person (you), and the third is third person (he, she, it, they), representing the conjugated forms for the personal pronouns of Spanish as shown on the right. Notice that the voseo form (used in certain regions of Latin America) appears in parentheses when it differs

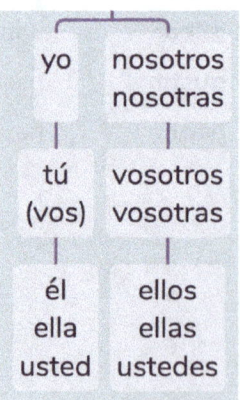

from the tú form (specifically in the present indicative, present subjunctive, and affirmative imperative). And although the Spanish in the exercises and the accent on the audio is Mexican, the vosotros/as forms (used in Spain) are also given in the tables.

The imperative mood is sub-categorized as 'affirmative' and 'negative' since the second-person informal forms (for tú and vosotros/as) are different in the affirmative and negative. The order of the tables is nosotros/as (Let's __) in the first row; tú and vosotros/as in the second row; and usted and ustedes in the third row.

The participles have various uses, but their main use is to follow an auxiliary to form a compound tense. In this use, neither the present nor past participles agree in gender or number with its subject– the form invariably ends in -o. The present participle follows a conjugated form of estar to express a continuous aspect (estar hablando – to be speaking), while the past participle follows a form of haber to express a perfect aspect (haber hablado – to have spoken).

The Exercises

Each table is followed by a page of exercises. (In the print version of this book, the exercises appear on the back side of each sheet of paper intentionally, so that the table is out of sight while you attempt the exercises.)

There are three exercises (A, B, and C), each consisting of five sentences. Since vos and vosotros/as forms are regional, they do not appear in the exercises.

In exercise A, you should identify the key verb and think about its conjugation. Which mood and tense is it? Is it regular or irregular? Study its use in the sentence and try your best to understand the meaning of the sentence and translate (either on paper or in your head) into English. You may find words in the sentence that you don't know and can't translate. That's fine! When you check the translations in the answer key, you have an opportunity to learn some new vocabulary. Keep in mind that there is more than one way to translate any given sentence, so your translation may be a bit different, but that's okay as long as the meaning is the same.

In exercise B, each sentence is presented with two forms of the key verb. Only one works in the sentnece. The other is either a non-existent, incorrect conjugation, or a conjugation that doesn't fit logically into the sentence (wrong person or tense). Again, try to translate or understand the complete sentence as best you can, and then check in the answer key.

In exercise C, a blank replaces the key verb. You need to come up with the correct conjugated form that matches the meaning shown by the English translation that follows.

In the audio tracks for the exercises, the correct forms of all sentences are read out, so you can also play the audio sentence by sentence to check your answers.

The Audio

You can stream or download the free accomanying audio tracks at www.lingualism.com/nksv1.

Each of the fifty key verbs has two tracks:

- the conjugation table
- the answers to the exercises

Check out our full catalogue of language learning materials at www.lingualism.com/shop

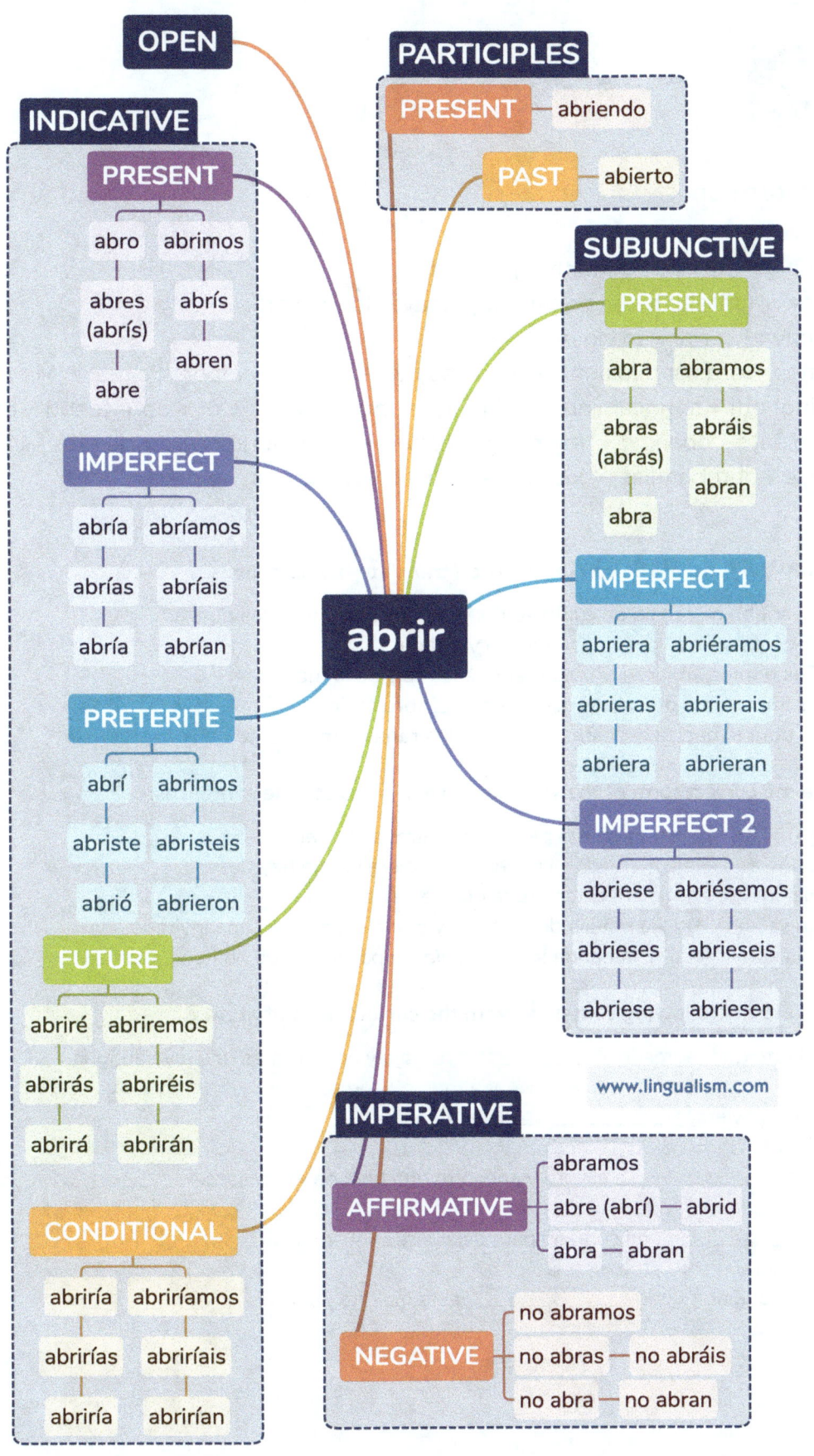

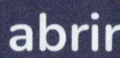
abrir

to open; to turn on

regular -ir verb

- o abrir algo – to open something
- o abrirse – (intransitive) to open (up); (leave) to take off
- o (antonym) cerrar – to close
- o (related words and idioms) • ¡Abre, soy yo! – Open the door. It's me! • ¡Me abro! –I'm (taking) off! • abrir camino a – to pioneer, pave the way for • abrir fuego – to open fire • abrimiento – opening • reabrir – to reopen • en un abrir y cerrar de ojos – in the blink of an eye • abrebotellas – bottle opener • abrelatas – can opener

A. **Identify the form of the verb abrir. Then translate the sentences.**

1. Ayer abrí mi regalo de cumpleaños y encontré una muñeca nueva.
2. Si no estuviera lloviendo, abriría la ventana.
3. Tus primos abrieron el restaurante a las seis de la mañana.
4. Es importante que abras con cuidado el libro antiguo.
5. Al abrir la puerta del carro, encontré una rana en mi asiento.

B. **Circle the correct form of the verb abrir. Then translate the sentences.**

1. ¿Abristes/Abriste la puerta para dejar entrar a los gatos?
2. Dudo que ella abriera/abre la puerta si supiera lo que hay detrás.
3. He abierto/abrido la ventana para que se salga el calor.
4. Luisa abró/abrió la botella de vino y sirvió una copa para cada invitado.
5. Ella aún abre/abra la tienda todos los días, a pesar de que no tiene clientes.

C. **Complete the following sentences with the correct form of abrir.**

1. Al rato que regreses _____ la caja y encontrarás una joya antigua.
   As soon as you return you will open the box and you will find an ancient jewel.
2. Si no lloviera, ¿_____ la ventana?
   If it didn't rain, would you open the window?
3. Ella _____ el libro y encontró una historia interesante.
   She opened the book and found an interesting story.
4. _____ mi corazón para dejar entrar el amor.
   I opened my heart to let love in.
5. ¿Por qué no puedo _____ esta maldita puerta?
   Why can't I open this damn door?

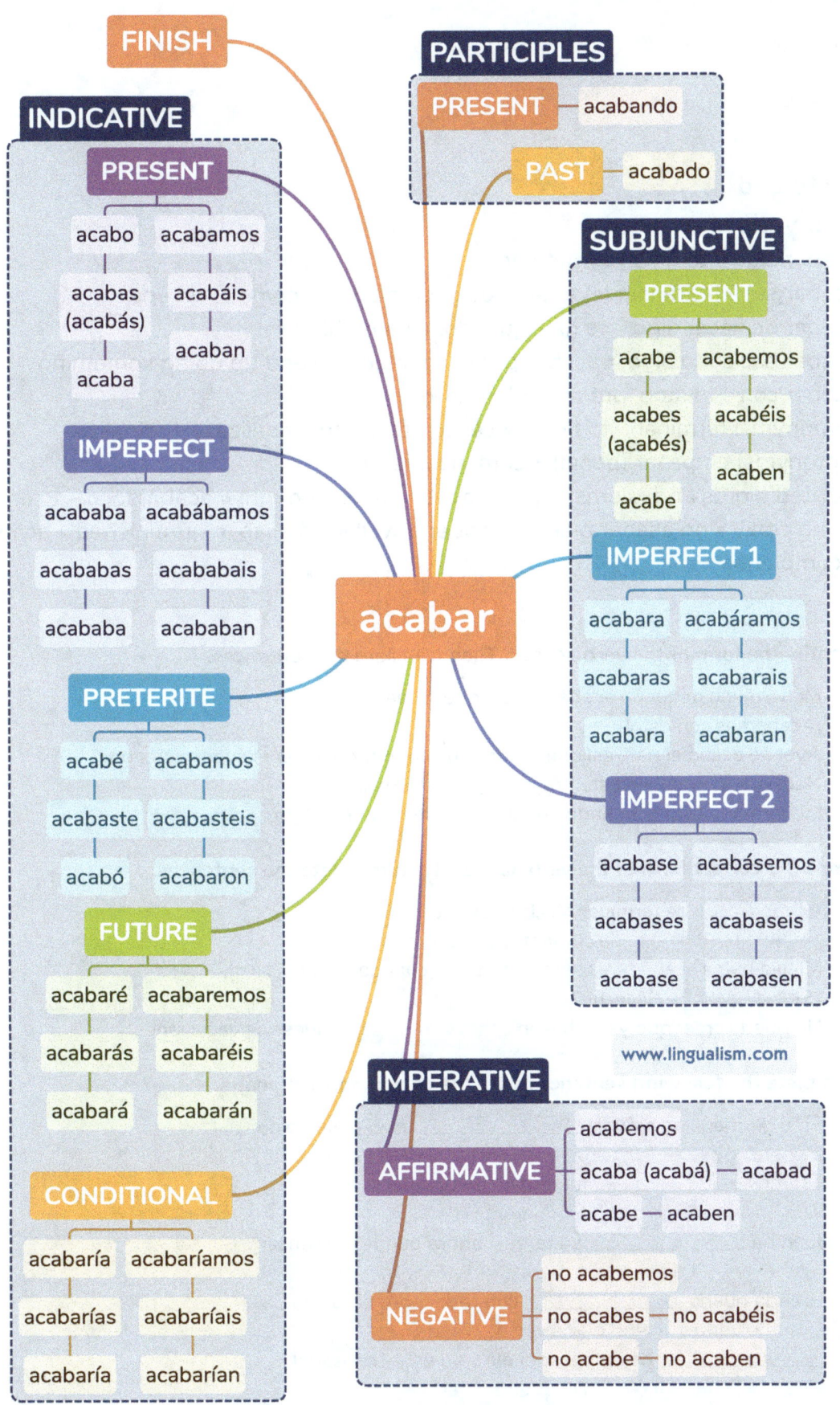

3 • Need-to-Know Spanish Verbs – Book 1

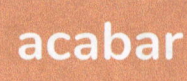

to finish; to end
regular -ar verb
- acabar algo – to finish something
- acabar(se) – (intransitive) to end, be over, be done, come to an end
- acabar de hacer algo – to have just done something
- acabar haciendo algo = acabar por hacer algo – to end up doing something
- acabar con – to stop, put an end to; to kill
- (synonyms) terminar – to finish • cesar – to cease • finalizar – to finalize
- (antonyms) empezar (begin) • comenzar (start)
- (related words and idioms) • ¡Se acabó! – That's enough! • acabar loco – to end up going crazy • no acabar bien – to not end well • sin acabar – unfinished • acabamiento – completion

A. Identify the form of the verb acabar. Then translate the sentences.
1. Mi hermano pequeño acaba de aprender a leer.
2. ¡Acabemos con esto!
3. Ayer se acabó el pan, así que tendré que comprar más en el supermercado.
4. Necesito que acabes este proyecto para el lunes.
5. Mi hermano está acabando su tarea en este momento.

B. Circle the correct form of the verb acabar. Then translate the sentences.
1. Acabe/Acabo de terminar mi libro favorito.
2. ¿Acabaste/Acábaste de comer toda la pizza?
3. Mi hijo había acabando/acabado su tarea cuando llegué a casa.
4. ¿Se acabó/acabió la leche?
5. No puedo creer que ya se hayan acabado/acabaran nuestras vacaciones.

C. Complete the following sentences with the correct form of acabar.
1. Si tu hermano no estudia _____ en el desempleo.
   If your brother doesn't study, he will end up unemployed.
2. Estimo _____ mi trabajo en una hora.
   I estimate to finish my work in an hour.
3. Juan ha _____ su tarea y ahora puede descansar.
   Juan has finished his homework and now he can rest.
4. Brenda quería _____ con todo, pero no podía.
   Brenda wanted to end it all, but she couldn't.
5. ¡_____ de empezar el día y ya estoy cansada!
   The day just started and I'm already tired!

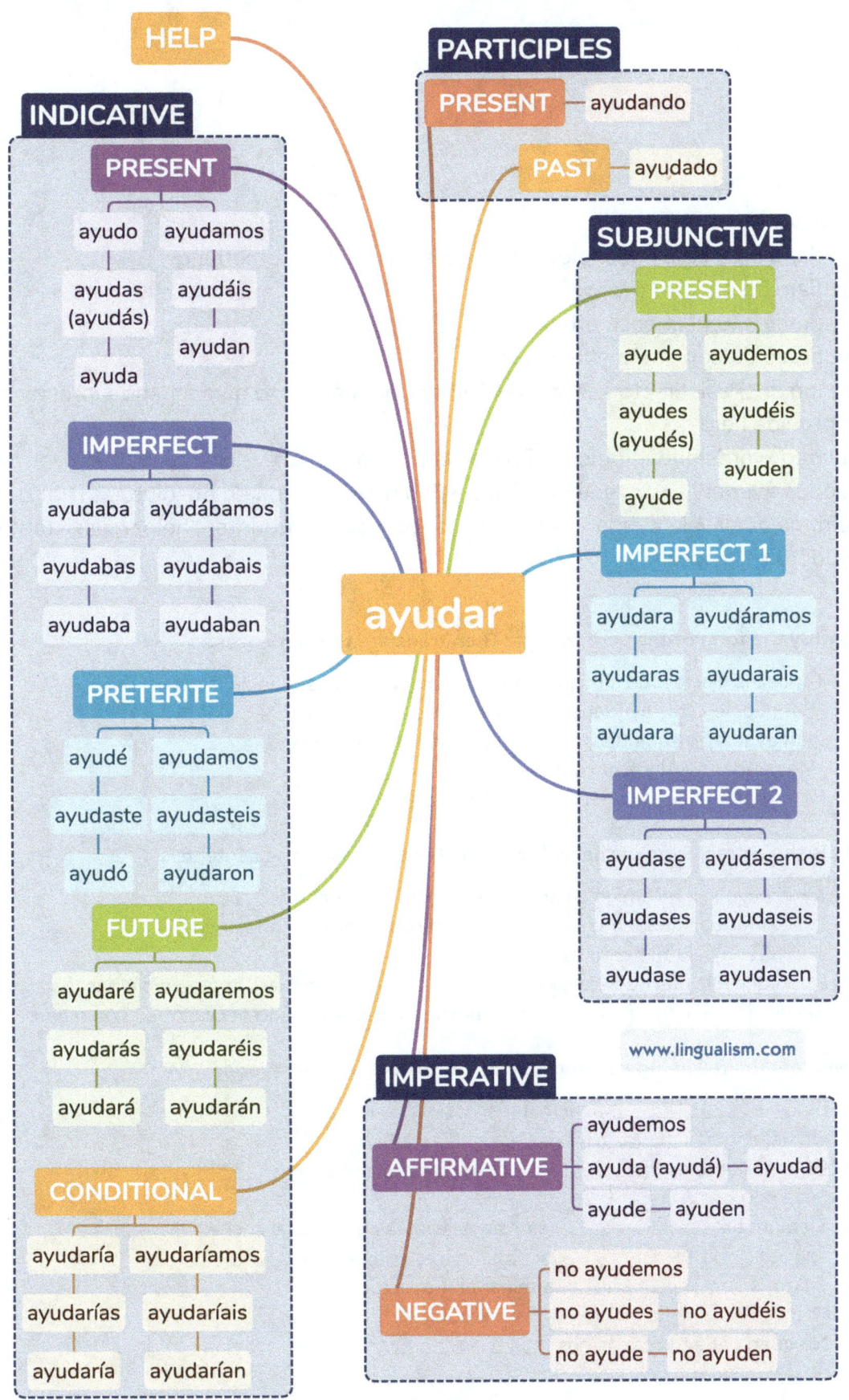

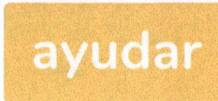

to help, assist, aid
regular -ar verb
- ayudar a alguien a hacer algo – to help someone do something
- ayudar con/en – to help with
- ayudarse – to help each other
- ayudarse de/con – to make use of
- (synonyms) asistir – to assist • dar/echar una mano – to give a hand • prestar ayuda – to provide help
- (related words and idioms) • ¿En qué le puedo ayudar? – How can I help you? • ¿Me puedes ayudar? – Can you help me? • Eso no me ayuda en absoluto. – That doesn't help me at all. • la ayuda – help, assistance • el/la ayudante – helper, assistant • ayudador – helpful

A. **Identify the form of the verb ayudar. Then translate the sentences.**
  1. Todos los días ayudo a mi hermano con sus tareas después de la escuela.
  2. ¿Por qué no estás ayudando a tu papá a reparar el carro?
  3. Juan ayudará a su abuela a hacer los mandados mañana.
  4. ¿Me puedes ayudar a encontrar mi libro?
  5. Es importante que ayudemos a los demás.

B. **Circle the correct form of the verb ayudar. Then translate the sentences.**
  1. Ayudí/Ayudé a mi amigo a cambiar la llanta de su coche.
  2. Luis y Martha ayudaban/ayudaron a su abuela a cocinar cada noche.
  3. ¡Ayuda/Ayude a tu hermana!
  4. Dudo que ella nos hubiera podido ayudar/ayudado si supiera lo que había pasado.
  5. Siempre ayudamos/ayudábamos a nuestros vecinos cuando necesitaban una mano.

C. **Complete the following sentences with the correct form of ayudar.**
  1. Estoy _____ a mi mamá a cocinar.
     I'm helping my mom cook.
  2. Es importante que _____ a nuestros amigos.
     It is important that we help our friends.
  3. Siempre he _____ a mi tía a llevar las maletas al coche.
     I have always helped my aunt carry the bags to the car.
  4. Ella va a _____ a terminar el proyecto.
     She's going to help you finish the project.
  5. No quería que tus papás nos _____.
     She didn't want your parents to help us.

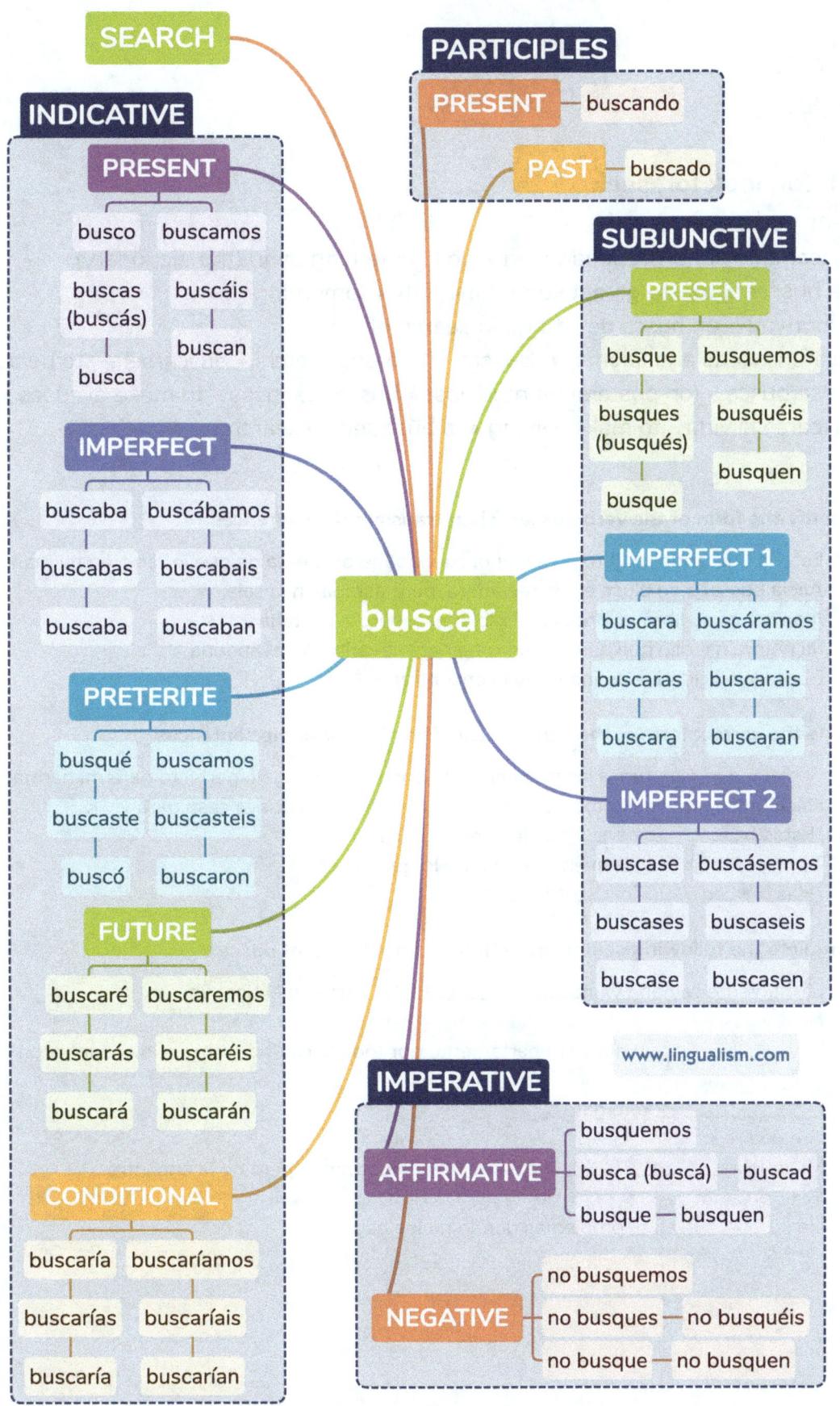

to search for, look for, seek
regular -ar verb; c → qu
- buscar algo en (el diccionario) – to look something up in (the dictionary)
- ir a buscar algo – to go get something, fetch something
- (synonym) ir en busca de – to go in search of
- (related words and idioms) • ¡Busca! – (to a dog) Fetch! • buscársela – to be asking for it • se busca – (on posters) wanted, lost • buscar excusas – to make excuses • buscarse la vida – to make a living • la búsqueda – search

A. Identify the form of the verb buscar. Then translate the sentences.
1. Estaba buscando mi libro de español cuando me di cuenta de que lo tenía en mi mano.
2. Alicia buscaba su blusa en mi recámara, pero estaba en la sala.
3. Juan buscó su libro favorito en la biblioteca, pero no estaba
4. Mi madre me dijo que buscara mi ropa para llevarla a la lavandería.
5. Busca la felicidad en tu interior y la encontrarás.

B. Circle the correct form of the verb buscar. Then translate the sentences.
1. Busqué/Busqué en todas las tiendas hasta encontrar el regalo perfecto para mi hermana.
2. Hace un año que nosotros buscamos/buscábamos una nueva casa para vivir.
3. ¿Estás buscas/buscando a alguien en particular?
4. Tú buscaste/buscas la aventura en todo lo que haces.
5. ¿Has buscado/buscando tus llaves?

C. Complete the following sentences with the correct form of buscar.
1. La siguiente semana vamos a _____ setas en el bosque.
   Next week we are going to look for mushrooms in the forest.
2. _____ un nuevo departamento por toda la ciudad, pero no lo encontraron.
   They searched all over the city for a new apartment but did not find one.
3. ¿_____ a tu gato?
   Are you looking for your cat?
4. Mi abuela _____ la palabra en el diccionario, pero no la encontró.
   My grandmother looked for the word in the dictionary, but she did not find it.
5. No _____ problemas donde no los hay.
   Do not look for problems where there are none.

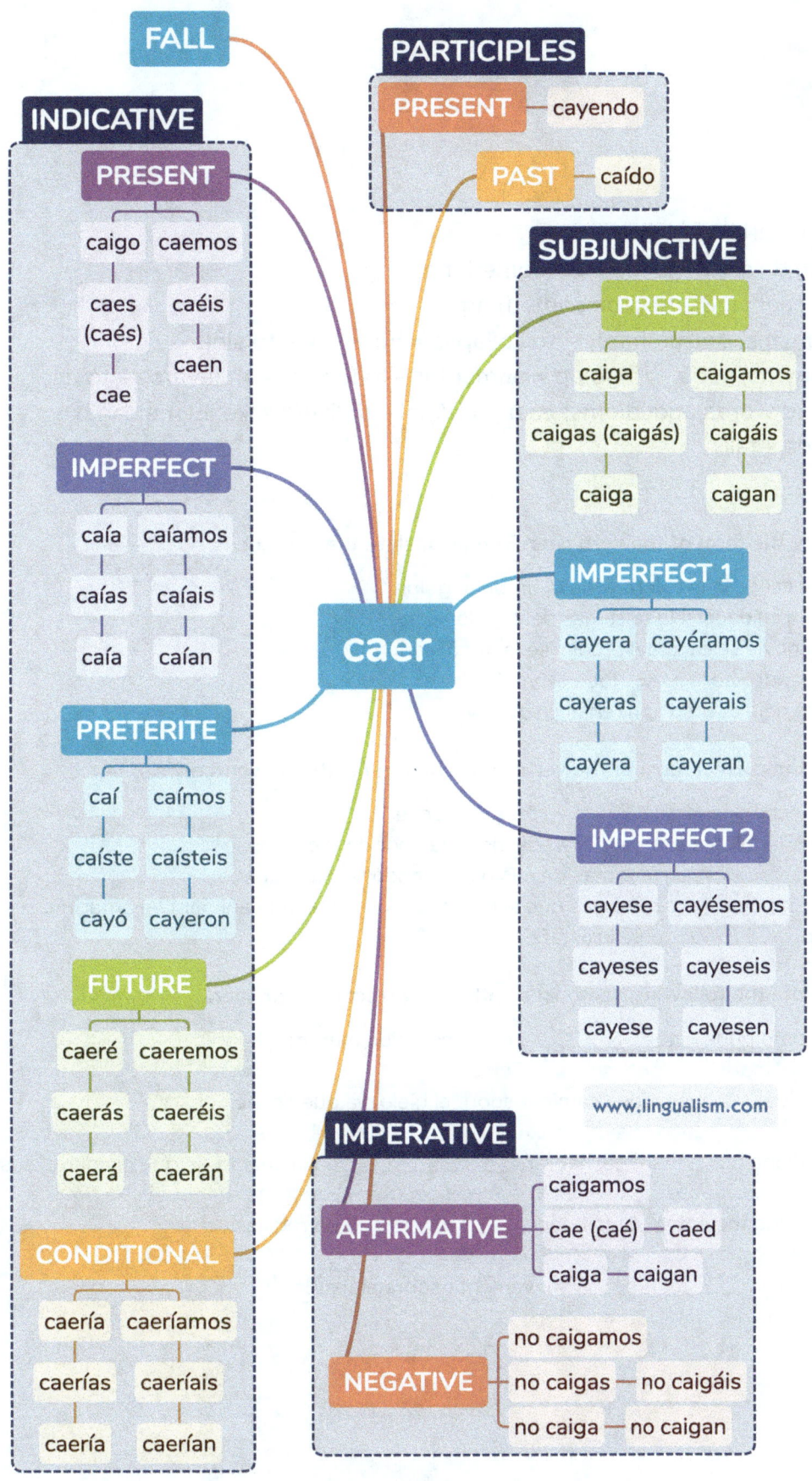

caer

to fall

irregular -er verb: caig-
- caerse de algo – to fall from something
- dejar caer algo – to drop something
- (synonyms) derrumbarse – to collapse • hundirse – to sink
- (antonyms) subir – to go up • aumentar – to increase • elevarse – to rise
- (related words and idioms) caer bien/mal – to like/dislike: Él me cae bien. – I like him. • la caída – fall

A. **Identify the form of the verb caer. Then translate the sentences.**
1. Me caí de la escalera y me di un buen golpe.
2. ¡Ten cuidado! ¡No te caigas del tejado!
3. Mi novia se cayó del árbol y se lastimó la pierna.
4. Cuando cae la nieve, todo se vuelve blanco.
5. Ella dejó caer su libro en el piso.

B. **Circle the correct form of the verb caer. Then translate the sentences.**
1. Anoche una rama caió/cayó sobre mi coche.
2. ¡Cuidado! Vas a te caer/caerte si no miras por dónde pisas.
3. Ayer cayeron/caí lágrimas de mis ojos cuando te dije adiós.
4. Mi papá siempre me decía que si me caigo/caía, él estaría ahí para levantarme.
5. No cayes/caigas en esa estafa.

C. **Complete the following sentences with the correct form of caer.**
1. ¿Cómo pude _____ en esa estúpida mentira?
   How could I fall for that stupid lie?
2. No fue una buena idea caminar sobre el hielo, ya que acabé _____.
   It was not a good idea to walk on the ice, as I ended up falling.
3. Mañana por la mañana, habrán _____ en la cuenta de que olvidaron sus libros.
   Tomorrow morning, they will have realized that they forgot her books.
4. Cuando me enteré de la noticia _____ de rodillas.
   When I heard the news I fell to my knees.
5. La lluvia _____ suavemente sobre el tejado.
   The rain fell softly on the roof.

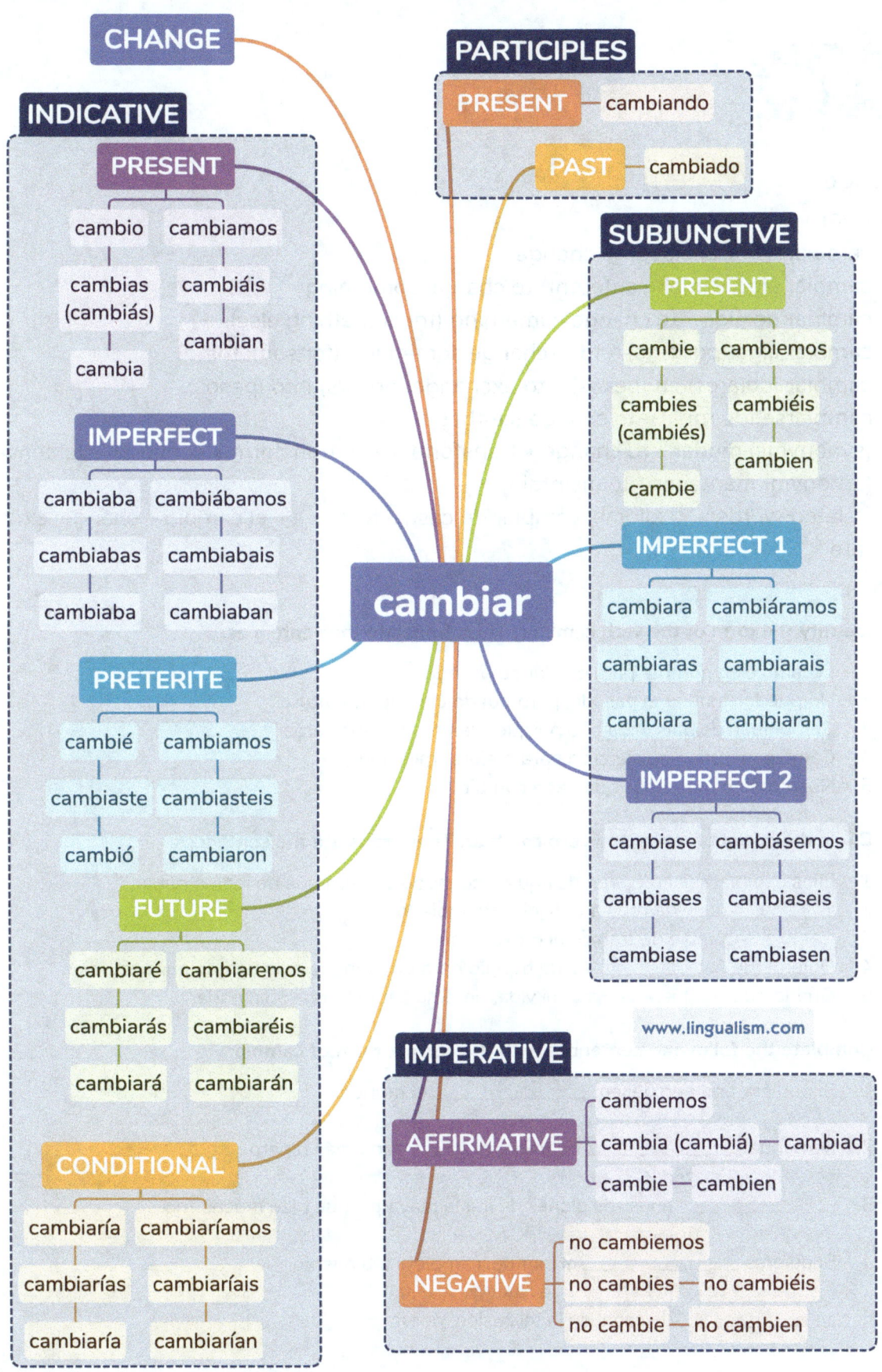

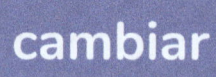

cambiar

to change

regular -ar verb

- cambiar – (intransitive) to change
- cambiar algo – (make different) to change something
- cambiar de algo – to change something (for something else)
- cambiar algo (por algo) – to exchange something (for something)
- cambiar (dólares) en (pesos) – to exchange (dollars) into (pesos)
- cambiarse (de ropa) – to change (clothes)
- (synonyms) mudar – to change • transformar – to transform • convertir – to convert
- (antonym) mantener – to maintain
- (related words and idioms) cambiar de casa – to move • el cambio – change; exchange rate

A. **Identify the form of the verb cambiar. Then translate the sentences.**

1. Él cambió su nombre para olvidar su pasado.
2. No puedo cambiar el pasado, pero puedo cambiar mi futuro.
3. Cambiaban de país cada año porque eran muy aventureros.
4. Cambié mi rutina de ejercicio para mejorar mi salud.
5. Nosotros no queremos que nada cambie.

B. **Circle the correct form of the verb cambiar. Then translate the sentences.**

1. Ellos cambiarán/cambiaron de equipo cuando supieron que no iban a ganar.
2. ¡Cambia/Cambie de ropa a tu hijo! ¡Está mojado!
3. Cambiaré/Cambié de trabajo el próximo año.
4. Quiero que cambias/cambies de trabajo para que tengas más tiempo para estudiar.
5. Quería que cambiara/cambió mi vida, pero no cambiara/cambió nada.

C. **Complete the following sentences with the correct form of cambiar.**

1. Si pudiera pedir un deseo, _____ el mundo.
   If I could make a wish, I would change the world.
2. Fernanda _____ de trabajo y ahora gana más dinero.
   Fernanda changed jobs and now she earns more money.
3. _____ nuestros planes de ir a la playa porque hizo mucho frío.
   We changed our plans to go to the beach because it was so cold.
4. Si quieres _____ el mundo, cámbiate a ti mismo.
   If you want to change the world, change yourself.
5. _____ de canal en la televisión, por favor.
   Let's change the channel on TV, please.

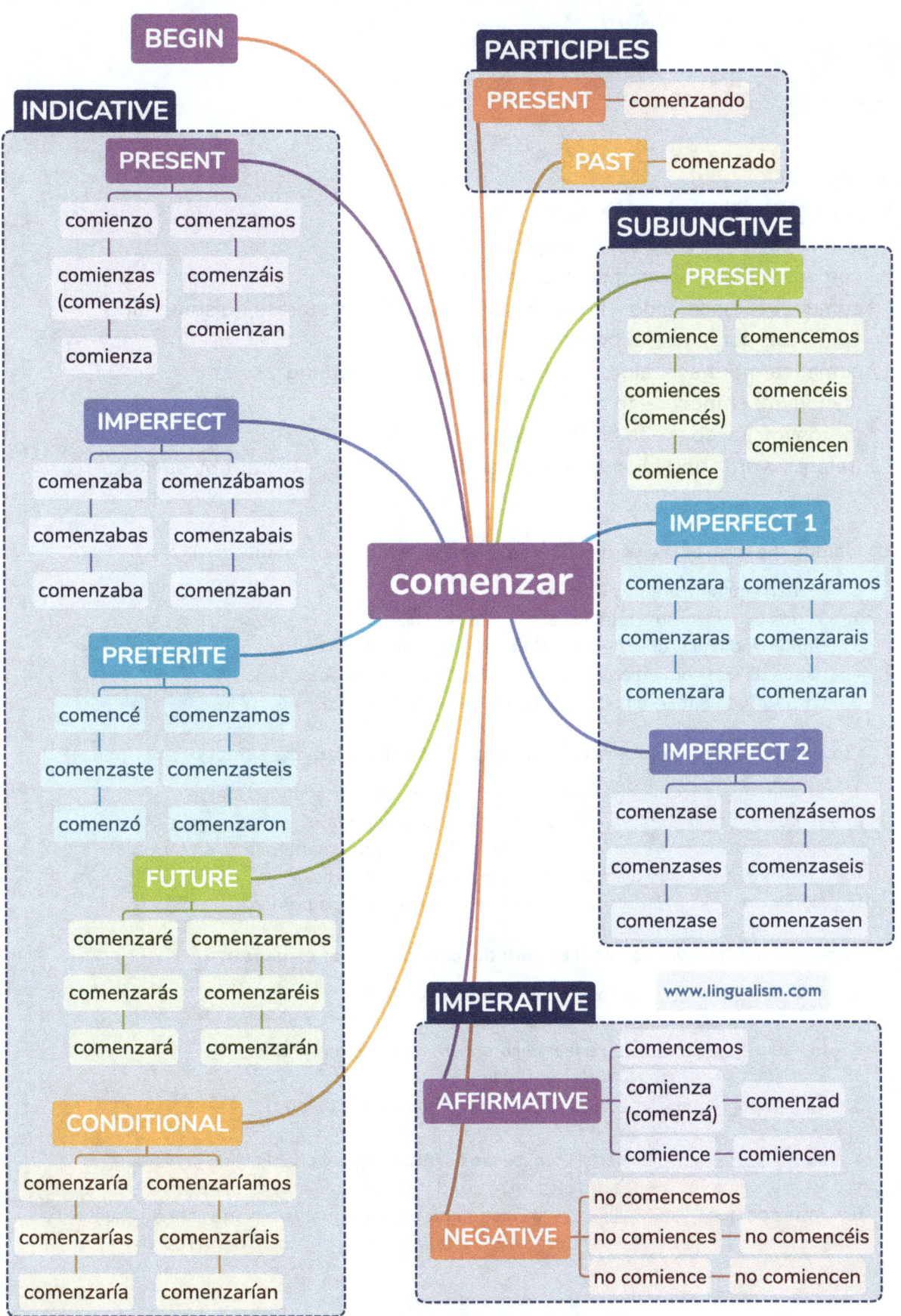

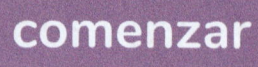

to begin, start

stem-changing -ar verb: e → ie; z → c
- comenzar – (intransitive) to begin, start
- comenzar algo – to start something
- comenzar a hacer algo – to begin doing something, start to do something
- comenzar por algo – to begin with something
- comenzar por hacer algo – to begin by doing something
- (synonym) empezar – to begin, start
- (antonyms) acabar – to finish • terminar – to finish
- (related words and idioms) comenzar diciendo que... – to start by saying...

A. **Identify the form of the verb comenzar. Then translate the sentences.**
   1. Mañana comenzaré mi nueva dieta.
   2. Todos comenzaron a reírse cuando conté el chiste.
   3. Comenzaría mi propio negocio si tuviera más dinero.
   4. Antes de que comenzáramos a hablar, supe que sería difícil.
   5. Desafortunadamente nunca comienzo mi tarea a tiempo.

B. **Circle the correct form of the verb comenzar. Then translate the sentences.**
   1. Si comenzaras/comienza tu día con una taza de café, te sentirías mejor.
   2. La pelea comienza/compenzó cuando tocan la campana.
   3. He comencido/comenzado a correr todos los días para mantenerme en forma.
   4. Comienza/Comenzó a llover justo cuando iba a salir de casa.
   5. Nunca comienza/comiences a correr sin calentar un poco primero.

C. **Complete the following sentences with the correct form of comenzar.**
   1. Ella _____ a llorar cuando supo la verdad.
      She began to cry when she learned the truth.
   2. Él había _____ a leer el libro, pero no pudo terminarlo.
      He had started to read the book, but he couldn't finish it.
   3. Es necesario que ella _____ a trabajar el día de hoy.
      She needs to start work today.
   4. Al _____ a leer el libro, se dio cuenta de que ya había leído la historia.
      As she began to read the book, she realized that she had already read the story.
   5. Antes de que _____ la clase, la profesora ya había pasado lista de asistencia.
      Before he started class, the teacher had already passed the attendance list.

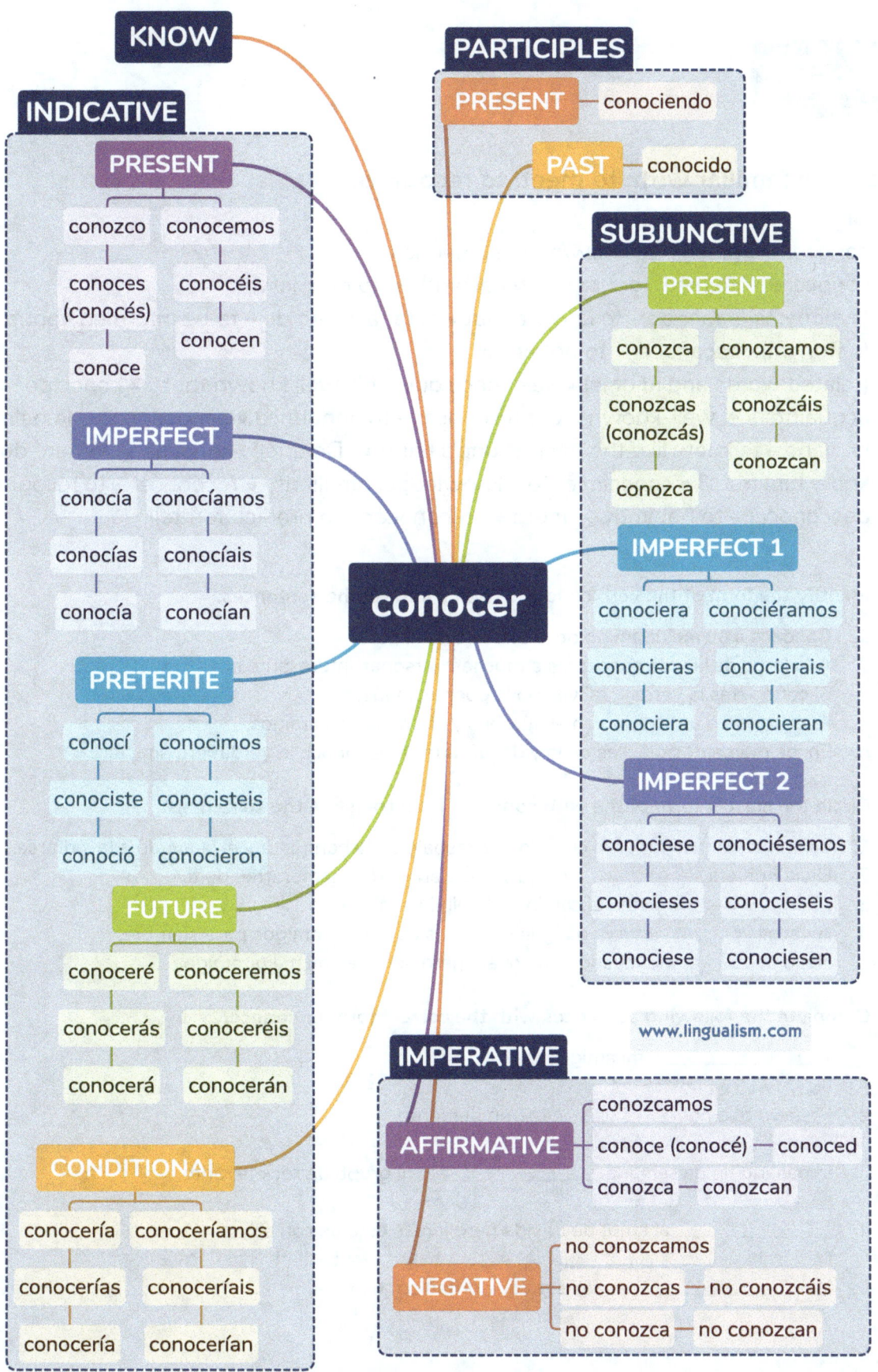

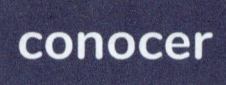

to know, be familiar with; to meet; to recognize
irregular -er verb; conozc-
- conocer a alguien – to know/meet someone
- conocerse – to meet, get to know each other; to be known
- (synonyms) saber de – to know about • estar al tanto de – to be informed about
- (antonym) desconocer – to not know
- (related words and idioms) • se conoce que – it's well known that… • conocido – acquaintance, well-known • dar a conocer – to announce • conocer como la palma de la mano – to know like the back of one's hand • ¿De qué lo conoces? – Where do you know him from? • conocimiento – knowledge, familiarity • reconocer – to recognize • desconocer – to not know, ignore • preconocer – to predict, foretell

A. Identify the form of the verb conocer. Then translate the sentences.
1. Conozco a mi mejor amigo desde hace cinco años.
2. A lo largo de la vida conocerás a muchas personas interesantes.
3. Si conocieras la verdad, tal vez no la podrías manejar.
4. Ayer conocí a un extraño en el autobús y ahora somos amigos.
5. En los momentos difíciles de la vida es cuando se conoce la verdadera amistad.

B. Circle the correct form of the verb conocer. Then translate the sentences.
1. Se conocieron/conocieran cuando ella resbaló en la banqueta y él la ayudó a levantarse.
2. Ojalá hubiera conocido/conocer la verdad antes de enamorarme de ti.
3. ¿Conoces/Conoce usted el camino a la biblioteca?
4. A veces conocen/conoces a alguien y sabes que serán amigos para siempre.
5. No lo conocía/conocí cuando era joven, pero ahora es mi mejor amigo.

C. Complete the following sentences with the correct form of conocer.
1. ¿_____ a mi amigo José?
   Do you know my friend José?
2. Prefiero que nos _____ en persona.
   I prefer that we meet in person.
3. El pasado fin de semana _____ a mi grupo de rock favorito.
   Last weekend I met my favorite rock group.
4. _____ al amor de tu vida pero jamás estarás con él.
   You will meet the love of your life, but you will never be with him.
5. Nos _____ en la fiesta que organizó tu prima.
   We met at the party your cousin threw.

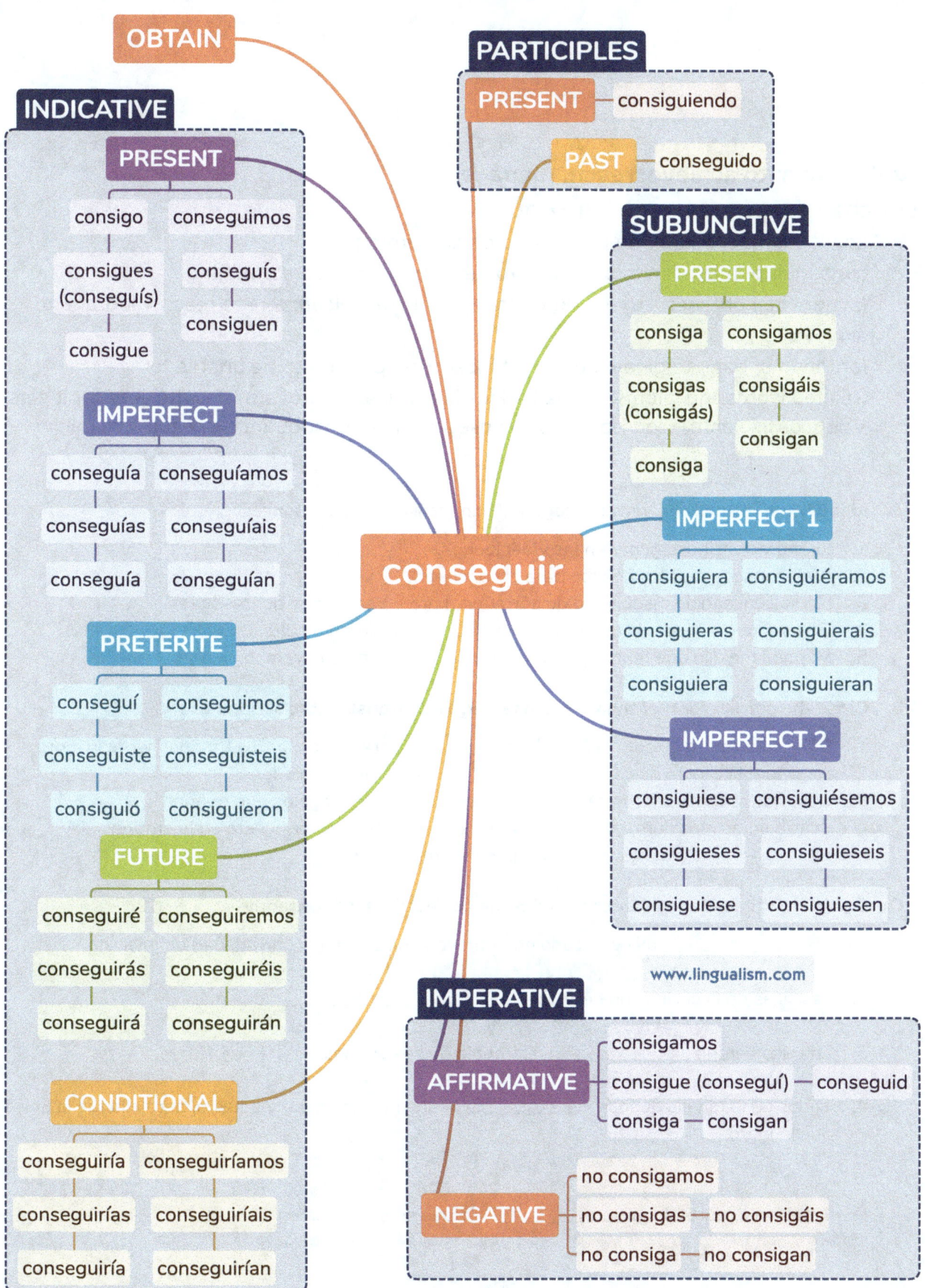

conseguir

to get, obtain; to achieve, reach, manage

stem-changing -ir verb: e → i; g → gu

- conseguir hacer algo – to manage to do something
- conseguir que alguien haga algo – to get someone to do something
- (synonyms) obtener – to obtain • tomar – to take • alcanzar – to reach • lograr – to achieve
- (antonyms) dar – to give • perder – to lose • no poder – to be unable to
- (related words and idioms) El que la sigue la consigue – (proverb) He who goes for it gets it • por consiguiente – consequently • consecuencia – consequence • seguir – to follow

A. **Identify the form of the verb conseguir. Then translate the sentences.**
  1. Siempre consigues ganar en los videojuegos.
  2. Ayer conseguimos los boletos para el concierto.
  3. Había conseguido mi objetivo de correr un maratón en menos de tres horas.
  4. Él siempre conseguía lo que quería, hasta que le pusieron un alto.
  5. Mi papá me dijo que tengo que conseguir un trabajo para el verano.

B. **Circle the correct form of the verb conseguir. Then translate the sentences.**
  1. Roberto siempre quiso conseguir/consiguiendo un trabajo en la ONU, y finalmente lo logró.
  2. Ha sido difícil, pero he consiguido/conseguido superar mis miedos.
  3. Cuando eran niños, siempre conseguían/consigieron los regalos que querían.
  4. Si trabajaras más duro, conseguirías/conseguiremos un mejor puesto en la empresa.
  5. Conseguí/Consigué dejar de fumar gracias a mi médico.

C. **Complete the following sentences with the correct form of conseguir.**
  1. Si _____ mi certificado en primavera, podría ir a la universidad en invierno.
     If I got my certificate in the spring, I could go to college in the winter.
  2. Las sillas de la cocina son hermosas. Ojalá que _____ dos más.
     The kitchen chairs are beautiful I wish you could get two more.
  3. En poco tiempo _____ el trabajo de mis sueños.
     In a short time I will get the job of my dreams.
  4. Todos en la familia querían _____ una invitación para la fiesta, pero ella fue la única que lo logró.
     Everyone in the family wanted to get an invitation to the party, but she was the only one who got it.
  5. Trabajando duro todos _____ lo que se proponen en la vida.
     By working hard, everyone achieves what they set out to do in life.

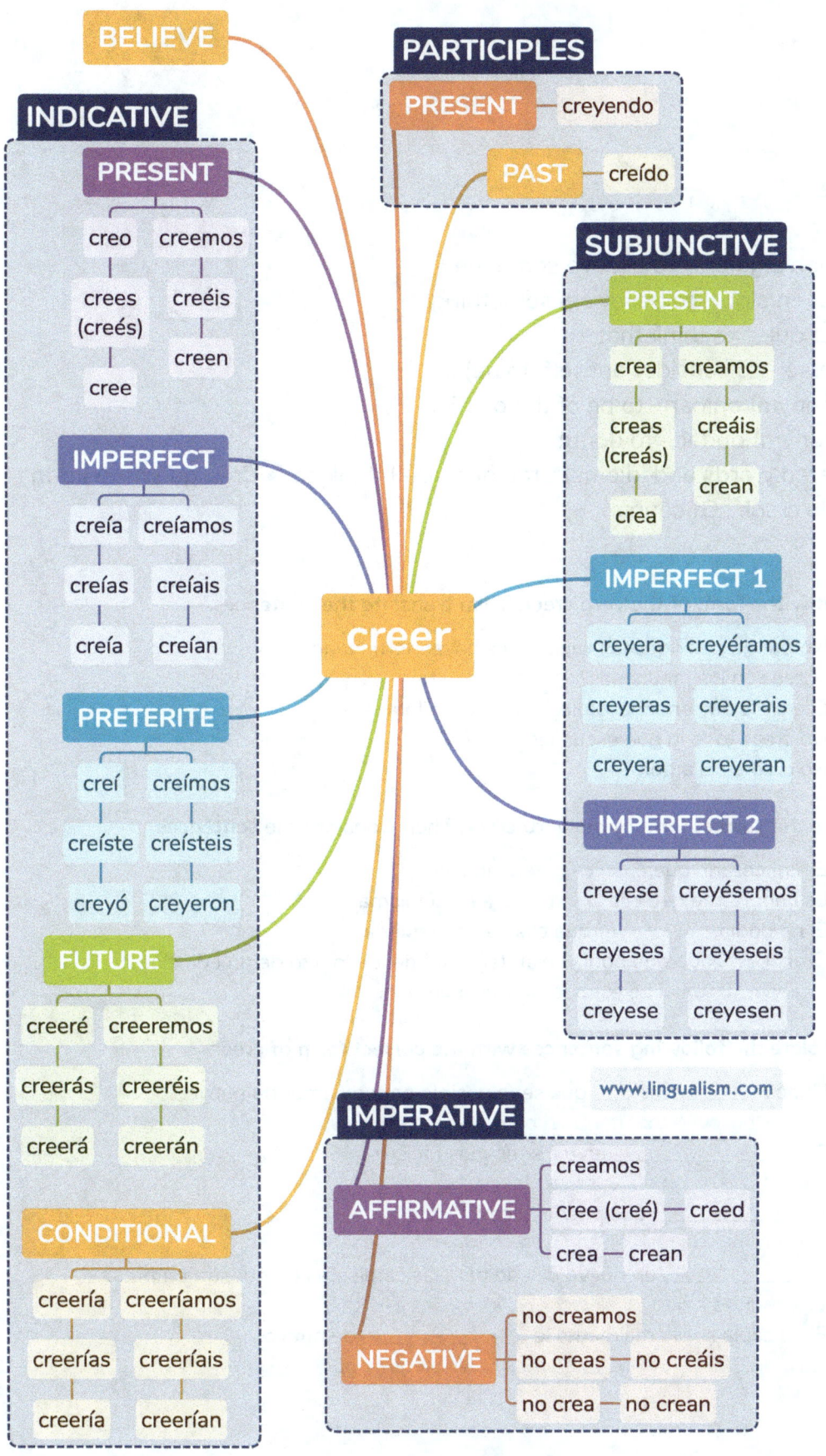

creer

to believe

regular -er verb

- creer a alguien – to believe someone
- creer en algo – to believe in something
- creer que – to think that…
- creerse – to consider oneself (to be)…
- (synonym) opinar – to be of the opinion
- (antonym) dudar – to doubt
- (related words and idioms) Creo que sí. – I think so. • Creo que no. – I don't think so. • ¡Ya lo creo! – Of course!

A. Identify the form of the verb creer. Then translate the sentences.
   1. No puedo creer que las vacaciones hayan terminado.
   2. ¿Crees en los fantasmas?
   3. Ella creía que era imposible, hasta que lo logró.
   4. No creas todo lo que escuches.
   5. No creo en el amor.

B. Circle the correct form of the verb creer. Then translate the sentences.
   1. Era necesario que él crea/creyera en ella.
   2. Es importante que ella crea/creyera en sí misma.
   3. Él no podía creído/creer que ella ya no lo quería.
   4. Creía/Creyendo que podía volar, (él) saltó desde lo alto de un edificio.
   5. ¡Créame/Créeme! Le estoy diciendo la verdad.

C. Complete the following sentences with the correct form of creer.
   1. Nunca _____ que sería posible para mí amar de nuevo.
      I never believed that it would be possible for me to love again.
   2. Si tú _____ en mí, sería más fácil.
      If you believed in me, it would be easier.
   3. ¿_____ que pueda hacerlo?
      Do you think I can do it?
   4. _____ un nuevo diseño para las camisetas de nuestra empresa.
      We created a new design for our company t-shirts.
   5. Él no sabía si ella realmente le _____ de nuevo.
      He didn't know if she would really believe him again.

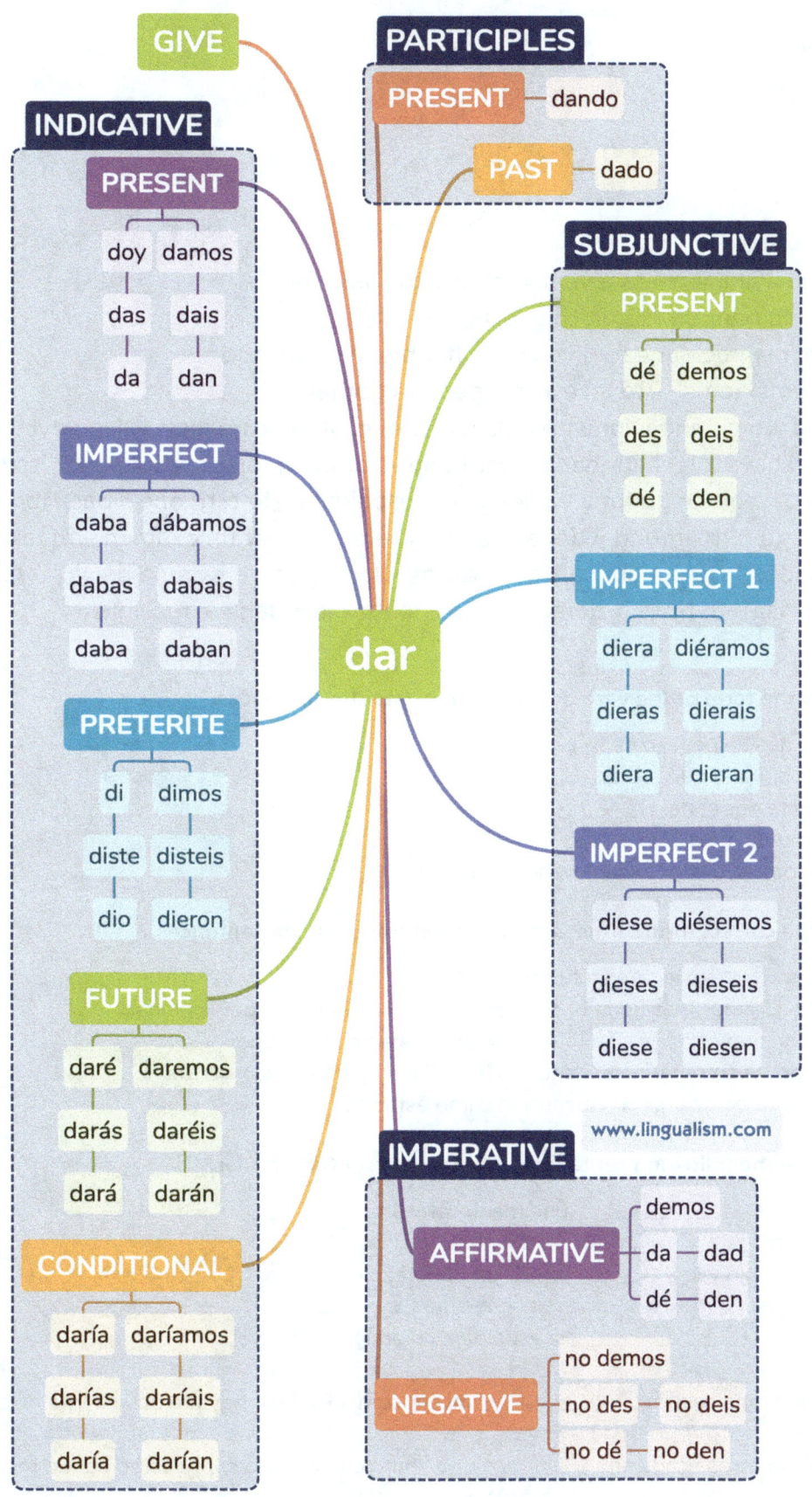

dar

to give

irregular -ar verb

- dar algo a alguien – to give something to someone
- darse – to happen, occur; to give up
- (synonyms) regalar – to give as a gift • prestar – to lend
- (antonyms) tomar – to take • recoger – to gather
- (related words and idioms) Me da igual. – I couldn't care less. • ¡No doy! – Duh! • Me da que… - I have a feeling that… • dar fe de – to vouch for • dar un paso – to take a step • dar un paseo – to go for a walk • dar la espalda a – to turn one's back to/on • dar la vuelta – to turn around • dar a luz – to give birth • dar un examen – to take an exam • dar conocer – to announce • dar gracias – to say grace • darse de alta – to register • darse prisa – to hurry • darse cuenta – to realize • dable – feasible

A. **Identify the form of the verb dar. Then translate the sentences.**

1. ¿Me das un pedazo de tu pastel?
2. Es mejor dar que recibir.
3. ¡No me des nada!
4. Mi mamá me dio un abrazo.
5. La doctora dará una conferencia mañana.

B. **Circle the correct form of the verb dar. Then translate the sentences.**

1. ¿Le daste/diste la tarea a tu profesora?
2. Si tuviéramos más tiempo, daríamos/diéramos un paseo por la ciudad.
3. Mañana voy a darte/dándote una manzana en el desayuno.
4. Luego de entregarme el paquete, (ella) dayó/dio la vuelta y se fue.
5. Siempre damos/dando nuestro máximo esfuerzo.

C. **Complete the following sentences with the correct form of dar.**

1. ¿Puedes _____ una mano con esto?
   Can you give me a hand with this?
2. Me empujó y le _____ un puñetazo en la cara.
   She pushed me away, and I punched her in the face.
3. Nunca le _____ la espalda a un amigo.
   Never turn your back on a friend.
4. Cuando me casé le _____ mi corazón a Pedro y hoy me doy cuenta de que fue un error.
   When I got married, I gave my heart to Pedro and today I realize that it was a mistake.
5. En la empresa cada año _____ una conferencia sobre cómo ser un mejor líder.
   In the company, every year they gave a conference on how to be a better leader.

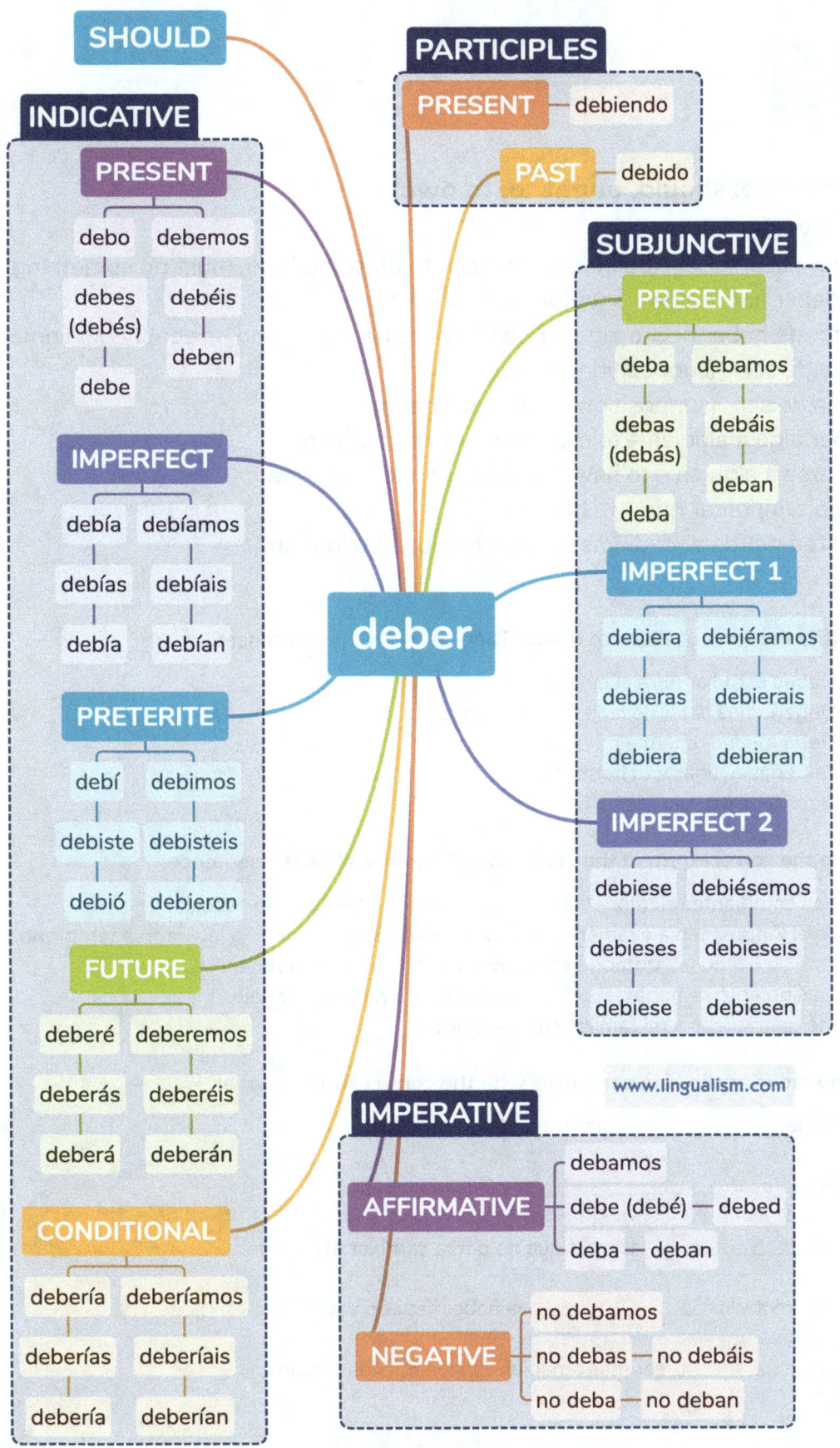

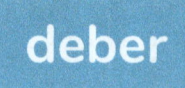

deber

must, to have to; should, ought to; to owe
regular -er verb
- deber hacer algo – (obligation) to have to do something, must do something
- no deber hacer algo – shouldn't do something
- deber de haber hecho algo – must have done something, probably did something
- debe de ser – (supposition) must be
- debía de ser– (supposition) must have been
- deber algo a alguien – to owe someone something
- deberse a alguien – to have an obligation to someone
- (synonym) tener que – to have to
- (related words and idioms) el deber – duty, obligation

A. **Identify the form of the verb deber. Then translate the sentences.**
  1. Debes estudiar para el examen.
  2. Deberíamos dejar de lado nuestros egos.
  3. Debo mucho dinero a mi banco.
  4. Deberías ayudar a tu hermano.
  5. Debí ser más cuidadoso, pero tropecé y caí.

B. **Circle the correct form of the verb deber. Then translate the sentences.**
  1. Los estudiantes siempre debrían/deben llegar a tiempo a la escuela.
  2. Ayer Andrés tenía examen a las 7 de la mañana y debe/debía levantarse temprano.
  3. Debiste/Deberías tratar de ser menos tímido con las personas.
  4. La siguiente semana deberás/debías buscar un nuevo trabajo.
  5. Me debo/diebo a mi familia y a mis amigos.

C. **Complete the following sentences with the correct form of deber.**
  1. No le _____ nada a nadie.
     I do not owe anybody anything.
  2. El profesor _____ corregir los exámenes.
     The teacher must correct the exams.
  3. Él _____ aceptar que no podía cambiar el pasado.
     He had to accept that he couldn't change the past.
  4. Los invitados _____ de haber llegado ya.
     The guests must have arrived by now.
  5. _____ ser más amables con los nuevos vecinos.
     We should be nicer to the new neighbors.

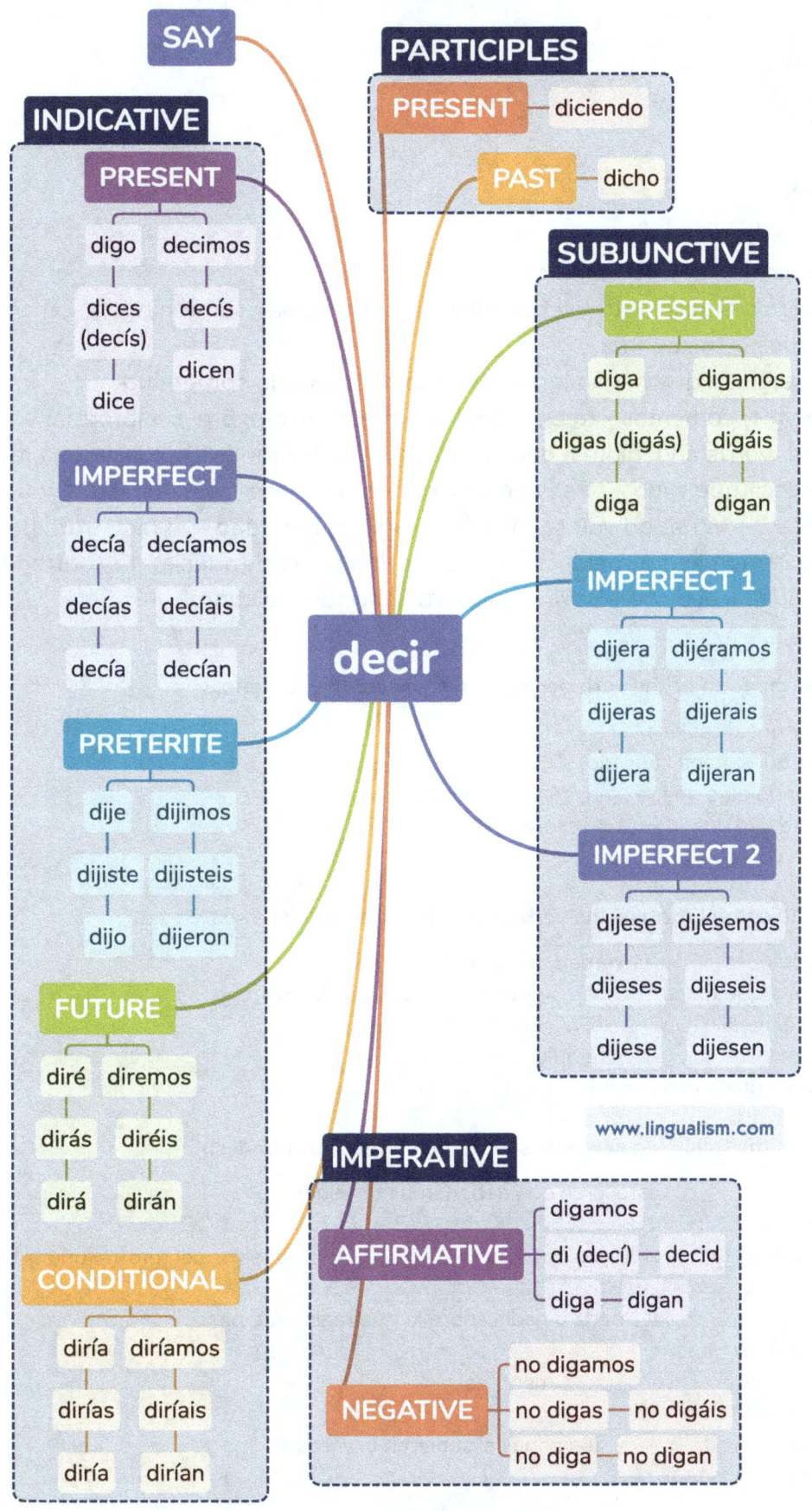

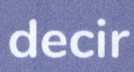

decir

to say; to tell

irregular -ir verb: dig-, dij-
- decir algo – to say something
- decir algo a alguien – to tell someone something, say something to someone
- decir que... – to say that...
- decir a alguien que haga algo – to tell someone to do something
- (synonyms) comentar – to comment • expresar – to express • informar – to inform
- (related words and idioms) decir la verdad – to tell the truth • decir una mentira – to tell a lie • decir que sí/no – to say yes/no • ¿Cómo se dice ___? – How do you say __? • ¿Tú qué dices? – What do you say (to that)? • a decir verdad – in fact, truth be told • bendecir – to bless • maldecir – to curse, damn • contradecir – to contradict • predecir – to predict • el dicho – saying, proverb • dicción – diction

A. **Identify the form of the verb decir. Then translate the sentences.**
1. ¿Por qué dices eso?
2. Dijo que estaba cansado.
3. Cuando digo que te amo, mi alma se estremece.
4. No te diré dónde está el tesoro.
5. Di la verdad a tu familia.

B. **Circle the correct form of the verb decir. Then translate the sentences.**
1. Si me deces/dices la verdad, te perdonaré.
2. Confío que todos digan/dicen que están de acuerdo conmigo.
3. ¿Qué me dijiste/dejiste? No entendí nada.
4. ¿Si te dijero/dijera que te quiero, me creerías?
5. No me gusta lo que estás dichendo/diciendo.

C. **Complete the following sentences with the correct form of decir.**
1. _____ esto, creo que deberíamos terminar.
   With that said, I think we should wrap up.
2. Teníamos tanta confianza que nos _____ nuestros secretos el uno al otro.
   We were so close that we told each other our secrets.
3. No _____ nada a nadie sobre lo que realmente pasó.
   I won't say anything to anyone about what really happened.
4. María, ¡no _____ mentiras!
   Maria, don't tell lies!
5. ¿Qué _____ tus papás si supieran la verdad?
   What would your parents say if they knew the truth?

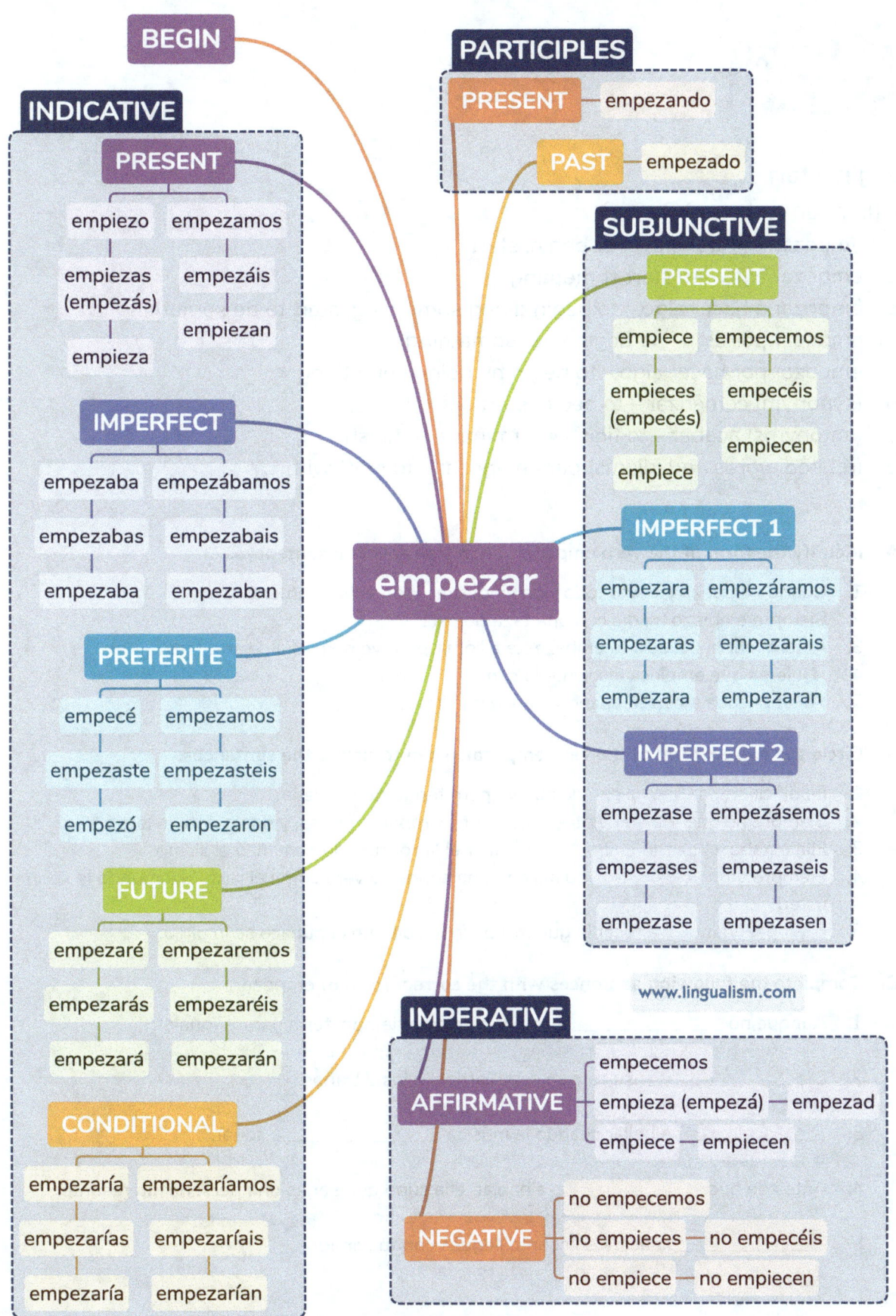

to begin, start

irregular -ar verb: e → ie; z → c

- empezar – (intransitive) to begin, start
- empezar algo – to start something
- empezar a hacer algo – to begin doing something, start to do something
- empezar por algo – to begin with something
- empezar por hacer algo – to begin by doing something
- (synonym) comenzar – to begin, start
- (antonyms) acabar – to finish • terminar – to finish
- (related words and idioms) para empezar – to start with, …;

A. Identify the form of the verb empezar. Then translate the sentences.
   1. Cuando empezó a nevar todos los niños corrieron a jugar afuera.
   2. Siempre empiezo mi día con una taza de café.
   3. Al terminar la película tú empezaste a llorar, pero yo no podía dejar de reír.
   4. ¿Quieres que empiece a cocinar la cena?
   5. Yo empezaba a correr, cuando comenzó a llover.

B. Circle the correct form of the verb empezar. Then translate the sentences.
   1. Es difícil empezar/empiezo de nuevo, pero tengo que hacerlo.
   2. Siempre he querido empezaré/empezar mi propia empresa, y finalmente lo logré.
   3. Ella estaba empezando/empezado a leer el libro, cuando comenzó el sismo.
   4. Siempre empieza/empiece su día con una sonrisa y verá cómo el resto del mundo le sonríe a usted.
   5. Él empezó/empizo a tocar la guitarra después de que el público se lo pidió.

C. Complete the following sentences with the correct form of empezar.
   1. Aunque no _____ a comer al mismo tiempo, terminamos iguales.
      Even though we didn't start eating at the same time, we ended up the same.
   2. Ella _____ su carrera como artista a los 21 años.
      She began her career as an artist at the age of 21.
   3. _____ a bailar cuando la música _____ a sonar.
      We started dancing when the music started playing.
   4. Antes de que _____ a hablar, ella supo que serías una persona interesante.
      Before you started talking, she knew you would be an interesting person.
   5. _____ la fiesta en cuanto llegues con tus amigos.
      We'll start the party as soon as you arrive with your friends.

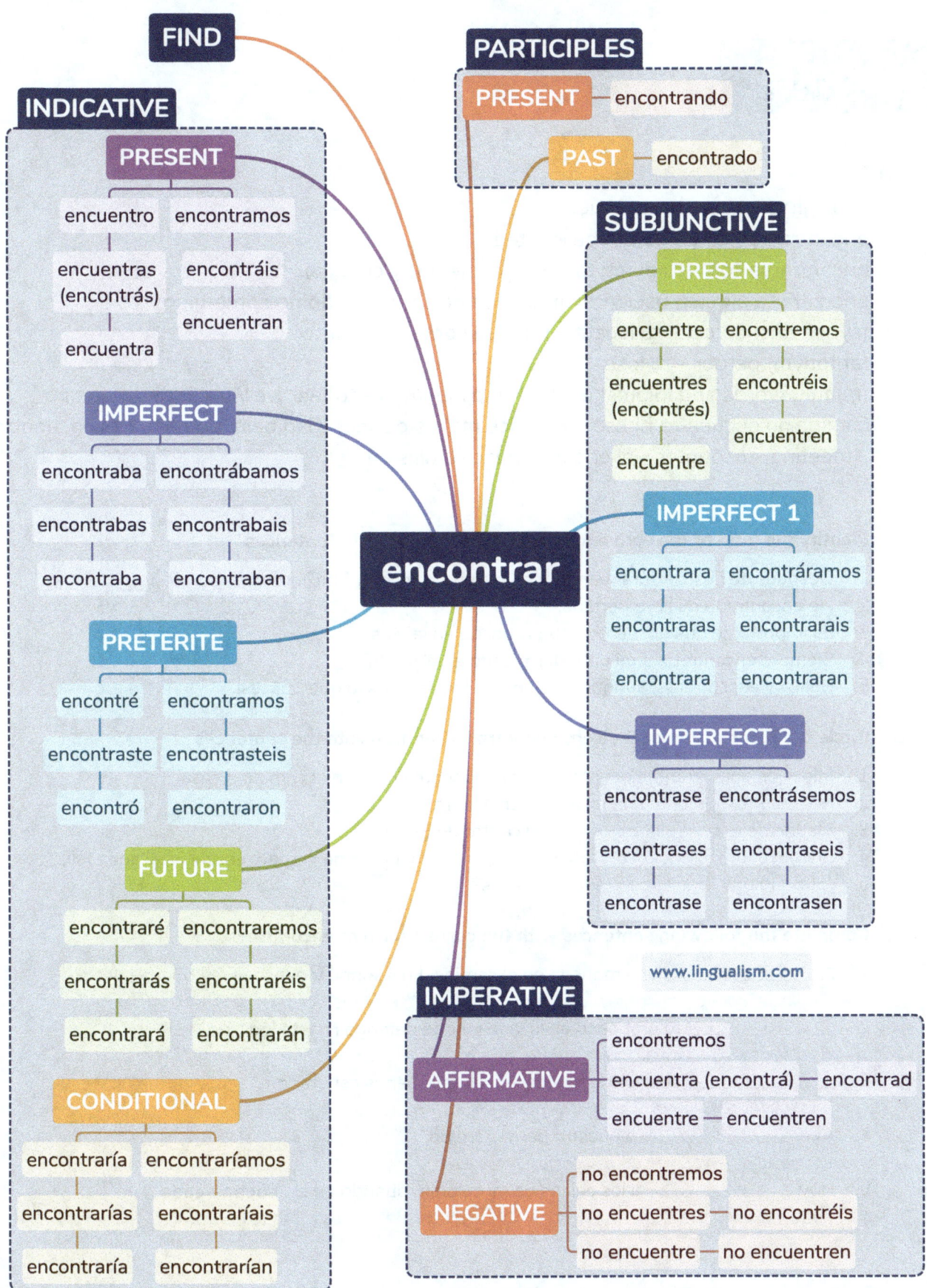

encontrar

to find

stem-changing -ar verb: o → ue

- encontrarse – to be found, be located
- encontrarse con – to meet; to run into, meet (by chance)
- encontrar a alguien haciendo algo – to find someone doing something
- (synonyms) ubicar – to locate • toparse con – to run into
- (antonym) perder – to lose
- (related words and idioms) encontrarse bien/mal – to feel well/ill • El perro que no camina no encuentra hueso – Practice makes perfect. / No pain, no gain. • el encuentro – meeting, encounter • el encontronazo – collision

A. **Identify the form of the verb encontrar. Then translate the sentences.**

1. Después de buscar durante horas en la tienda, encontré mi libro favorito.
2. He encontrado mi libro perdido.
3. Es importante que encuentres tu propósito en la vida.
4. Siempre encontraba a mi gato durmiendo en el jardín.
5. Busca y encontrarás, aunque no siempre encontrarás lo que buscas.

B. **Circle the correct form of the verb encontrar. Then translate the sentences.**

1. Mis hijos encontraran/encontraron una moneda de oro en el camino a casa.
2. Me encontré/encontrí con mi amigo en el parque.
3. Madrid se encontra/encuentra en el centro de España.
4. Si Juan encuentrara/encontrara una mujer que lo amara de verdad, entonces él sería feliz.
5. ¿Has encontradas/encontrado mis llaves?

C. **Complete the following sentences with the correct form of encontrar.**

1. Al _____ una moneda en el camino, Luis sonrió y pensó en su buena suerte.
   Finding a coin on the road, Luis smiled and thought of his good luck.
2. _____ tu propósito en la vida y no te detengas hasta lograrlo.
   Find your purpose in life and don't stop until you achieve it.
3. _____ el amor de tu vida en el lugar menos esperado.
   You will find the love of your life in the least expected place.
4. Ayer _____ a nuestro perro perdido.
   Yesterday we found our lost dog.
5. Hoy _____ a los chicos de mi colonia robando en el supermercado.
   Today I found the boys from my neighborhood stealing from the supermarket.

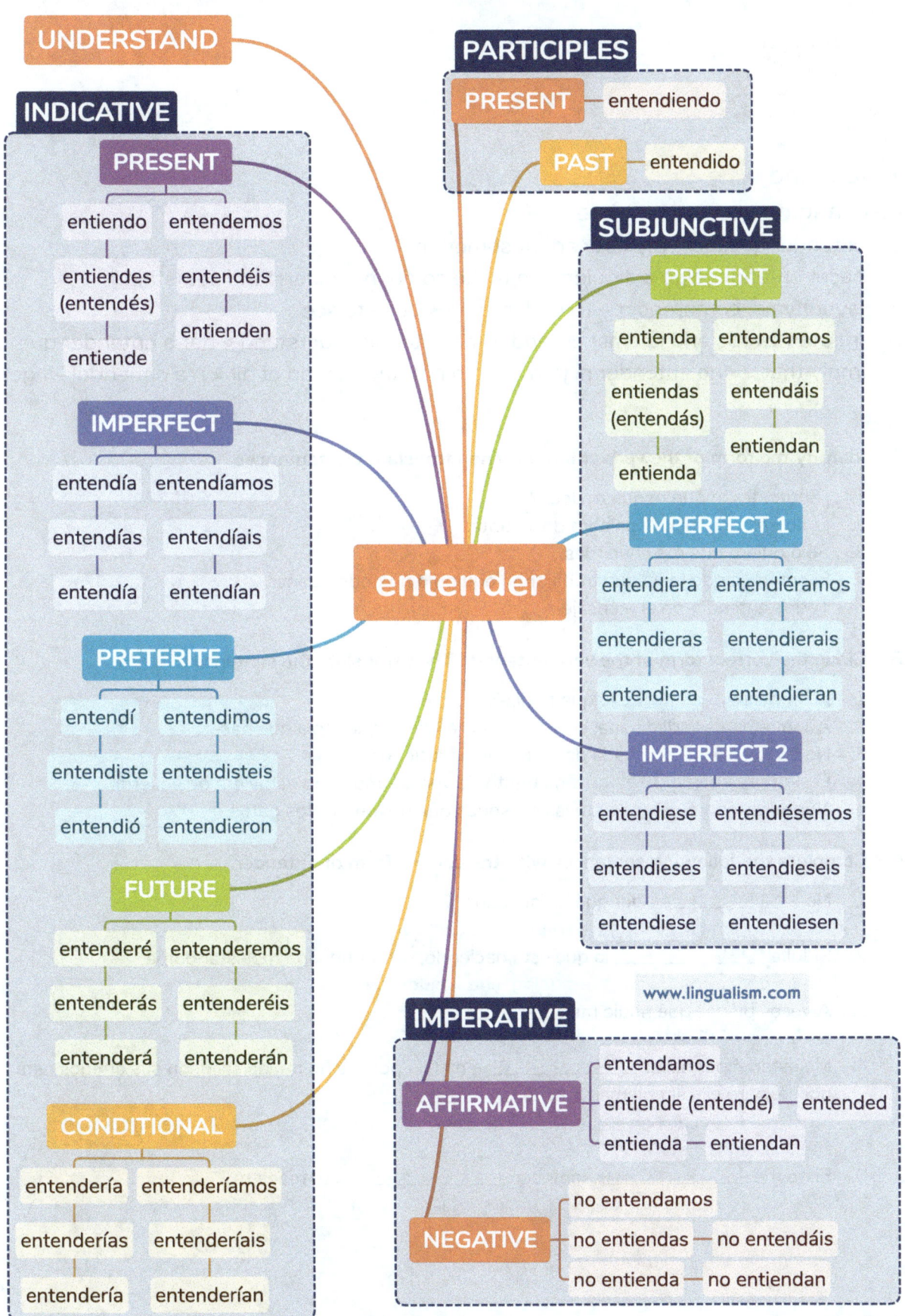

entender

to understand

stem-changing -er verb: e → ie
- entender de algo – to know about something
- hacer entender algo a alguien – to make someone understand something
- (synonyms) comprender – to understand • ver – to see
- (related words and idioms) entender mal – to misunderstand • dar a entender que – to imply that... • no entender ni jota de – to not understand at all • ¡Ya entiendo! – I get it!

A. **Identify the form of the verb entender. Then translate the sentences.**
   1. ¿Entiendes lo que te quiero decir?
   2. Él no entendió ni una palabra de la junta.
   3. Sólo quiero que me entiendas.
   4. Él entendía que tenía que trabajar en equipo o no podría ganar.
   5. Todos entendieron el mensaje.

B. **Circle the correct form of the verb entender. Then translate the sentences.**
   1. ¿Entendiste/Entiendiste lo que te dije?
   2. Aunque nadie le dijo nada, él entendó/entendió lo que tenía que hacer.
   3. No entiendo/entendo nada de lo que estás diciendo.
   4. Él siempre entendió/entendía mi punto de vista, aunque no estuviera de acuerdo.
   5. Nunca entendré/entenderé a las personas que no aman a los gatos.

C. **Complete the following sentences with the correct form of entender.**
   1. No _____ por qué hiciste eso.
      I don't understand why you did that.
   2. Si Julia _____ lo que está haciendo, no continuaría molestándome.
      If Julia understood what she's doing, she wouldn't continue to bother me.
   3. A veces pienso que nadie me _____.
      Sometimes I think nobody understands me.
   4. Me esforcé por hacer _____ a mi hija porque no puede salir con sus amigos esta noche, pero ella simplemente no lo _____.
      I tried hard to make my daughter understand why she can't go out with her friends tonight, but she just didn't get it.
   5. Si no me _____, tampoco _____ a tu maestra.
      If you don't understand me, you won't understand your teacher either.

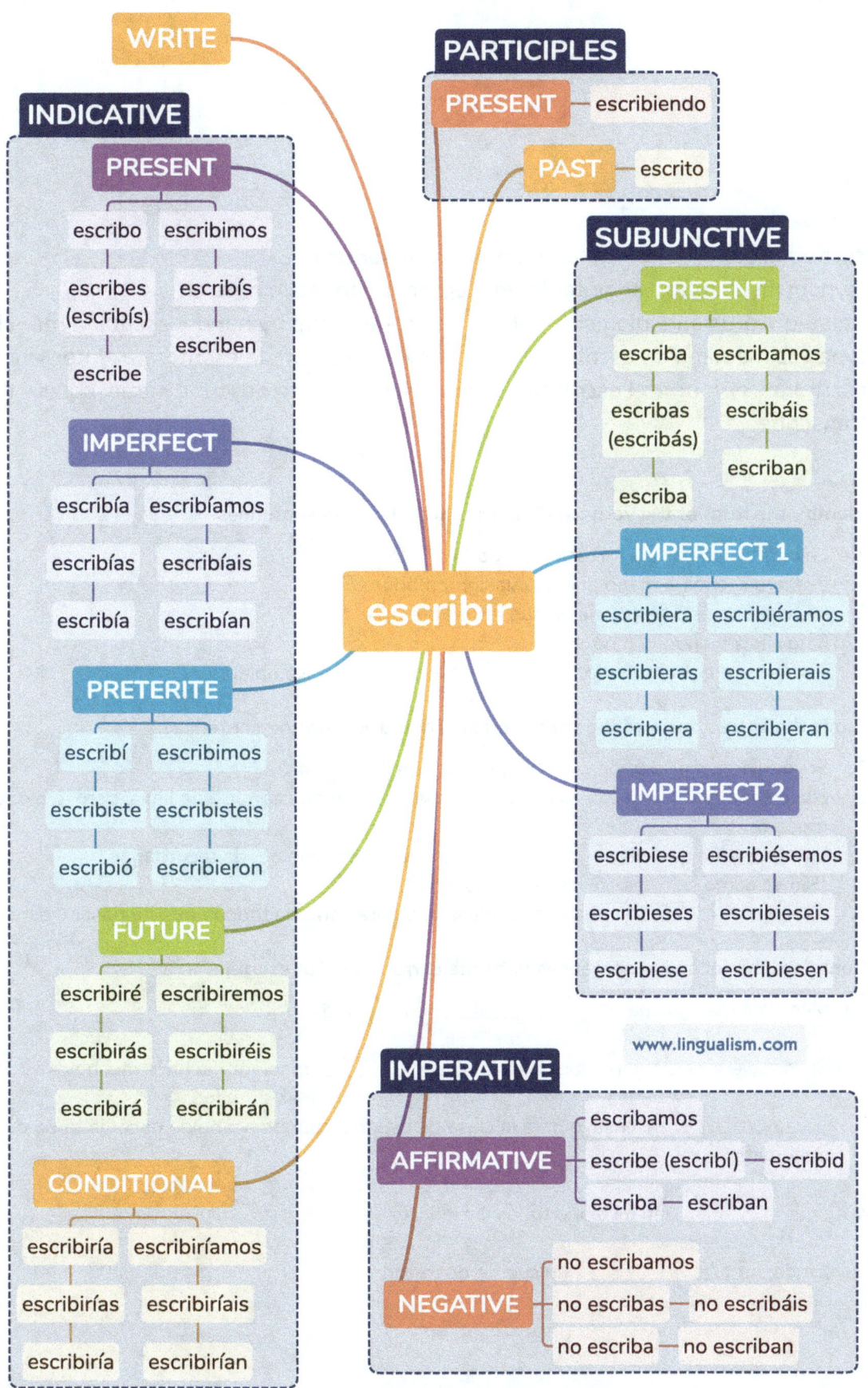

escribir

to write

regular -ir verb

- escribirse con alguien – to correspond with someone
- (synonyms) anotar – to note down • apuntar – to make note of
- (related words and idioms) escribir a mano – to write by hand • escribir a máquina – to type • la máquina de escribir – typewriter • el escritor / la escritora – writer • la escritura – writing • el escritorio – desk • describir – to describe • transcribir – to transcribe

A. Identify the form of the verb escribir. Then translate the sentences.

1. Le escribí una carta a mi mejor amigo.
2. Prefiero escribir a mano que usar la computadora.
3. Mi hermana escribe poesía en sus ratos libres.
4. Estoy escribiendo una novela.
5. Todos los días durante dos años, esperé a que ella me escribiera.

B. Circle the correct form of the verb escribir. Then translate the sentences.

1. Si yo tuviera más tiempo, escribiría/escribiré más cuentos.
2. Ella estaba escríbiendose/escribiéndose con un chico que conoció en línea, pero lo bloqueó por grosero.
3. Es importante que ella escriba/escribe sus ideas para que pueda recordarlas.
4. ¿Sabes cómo se escribe/escriben tu nombre en chino?
5. ¡Quiero escriba/escribir una carta a mi abuela para contarle todo lo que ha pasado este año!

C. Complete the following sentences with the correct form of escribir.

1. Mi mamá me dijo que no _____ en la pared.
   My mom told me not to write on the wall.
2. Si yo tuviera más tiempo libre, habría _____ mi biografía hace mucho.
   If I had more free time, I would have written my biography long ago.
3. _____ mi ensayo para la clase de español cuando acabe de hacer la tarea de matemáticas.
   I will write my essay for Spanish class when I finish my math homework.
4. _____ en mi diario todos los días.
   I write in my diary every day.
5. ¡Linda, no _____ un cuento de terror!
   Linda, don't write a horror story!

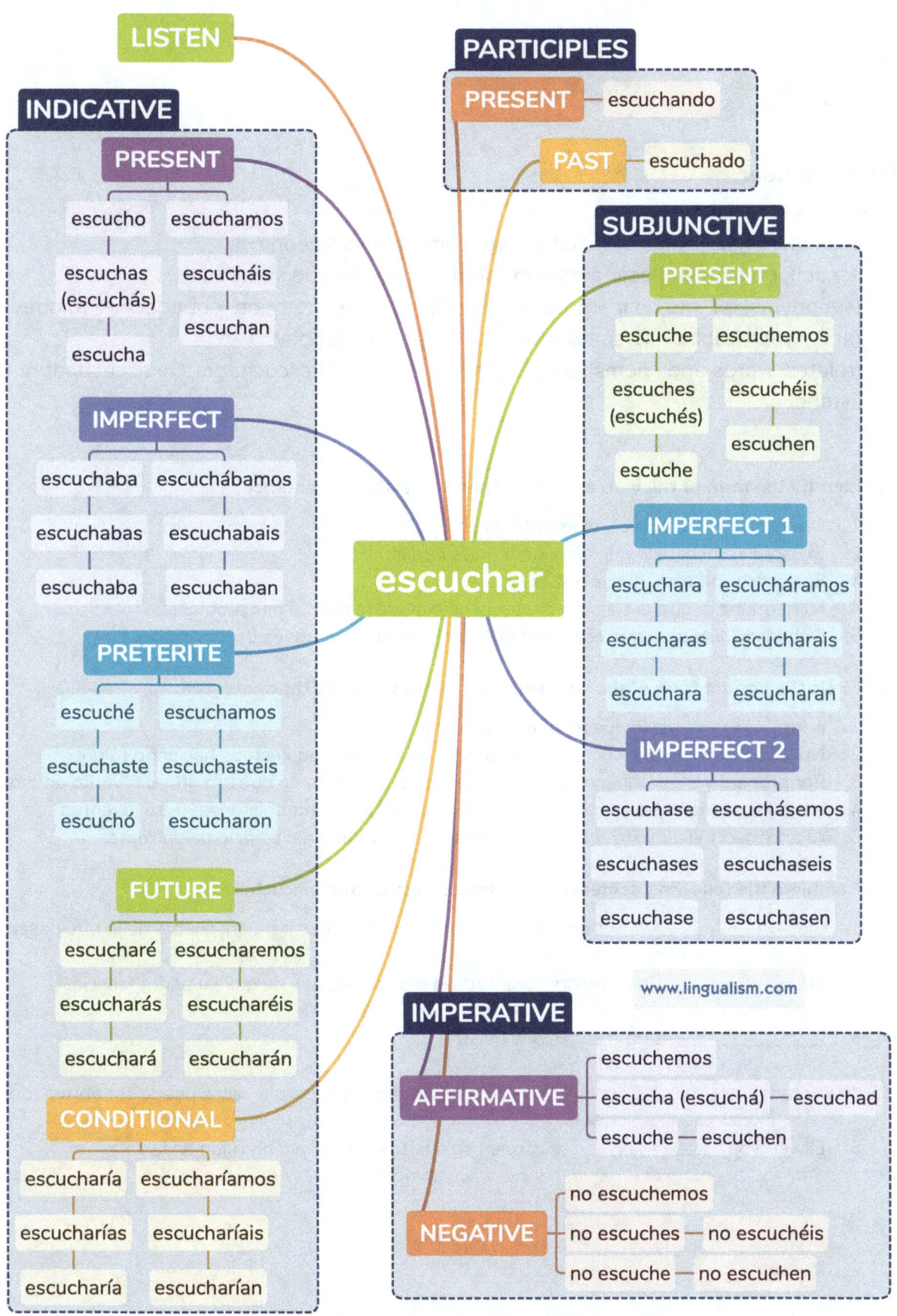

escuchar

to listen; to hear
regular -ar verb
- escuchar algo / a alguien – to listen to something/someone
- escuchar a alguien hacer algo – to listen to someone do something
- (synonyms) oír – to hear • prestar atención – to pay attention • obedecer – to obey
- (antonyms) hablar – to speak • desobedecer – to disobey
- (related words and idioms) la escucha – listening • el escuchador / la escuchadora – listener

A. **Identify the form of the verb escuchar. Then translate the sentences.**
1. Cuando escucho música, me siento feliz.
2. Si usted escuchara lo que digo, no tendría dudas.
3. Sí, escuchaste bien: te dije que te callaras.
4. Mi hermana pequeña siempre me escucha cuando le cuento mis problemas.
5. Deben callarse para que escuchen el sonido del viento a través de los árboles.

B. **Circle the correct form of the verb escuchar. Then translate the sentences.**
1. ¡Escuche/Escucha! No quiero verte nunca más.
2. No pude escuchado/escuchar la película porque mi hermano estaba haciendo ruido.
3. Por primera vez escucharamos/escucharemos el concierto de nuestro grupo favorito en directo.
4. Mis hijos siempre escuchaban/escucharon a su abuela contar historias de su juventud.
5. Al anochecer ella escuchó/escuchió gritos que provenían del edificio de enfrente.

C. **Complete the following sentences with the correct form of escuchar.**
1. Siempre _____ las conversaciones a escondidas para enterarme de lo que pasaba.
   She always eavesdropped on conversations to find out what was going on.
2. Él _____ a su madre llorar toda la noche después de que su padre falleció.
   He heard his mother cry all night after his father passed away.
3. _____ lo que tengas que decir.
   I'll listen to what you have to say.
4. Aprender a _____ a los demás es interesante, pero a veces puede ser abrumador.
   Learning to listen to others is interesting, but it can be overwhelming at times.
5. Ella estaba _____ música en su cuarto cuando oyó un ruido en la sala.
   She was listening to music in her room when she heard a noise in the living room.

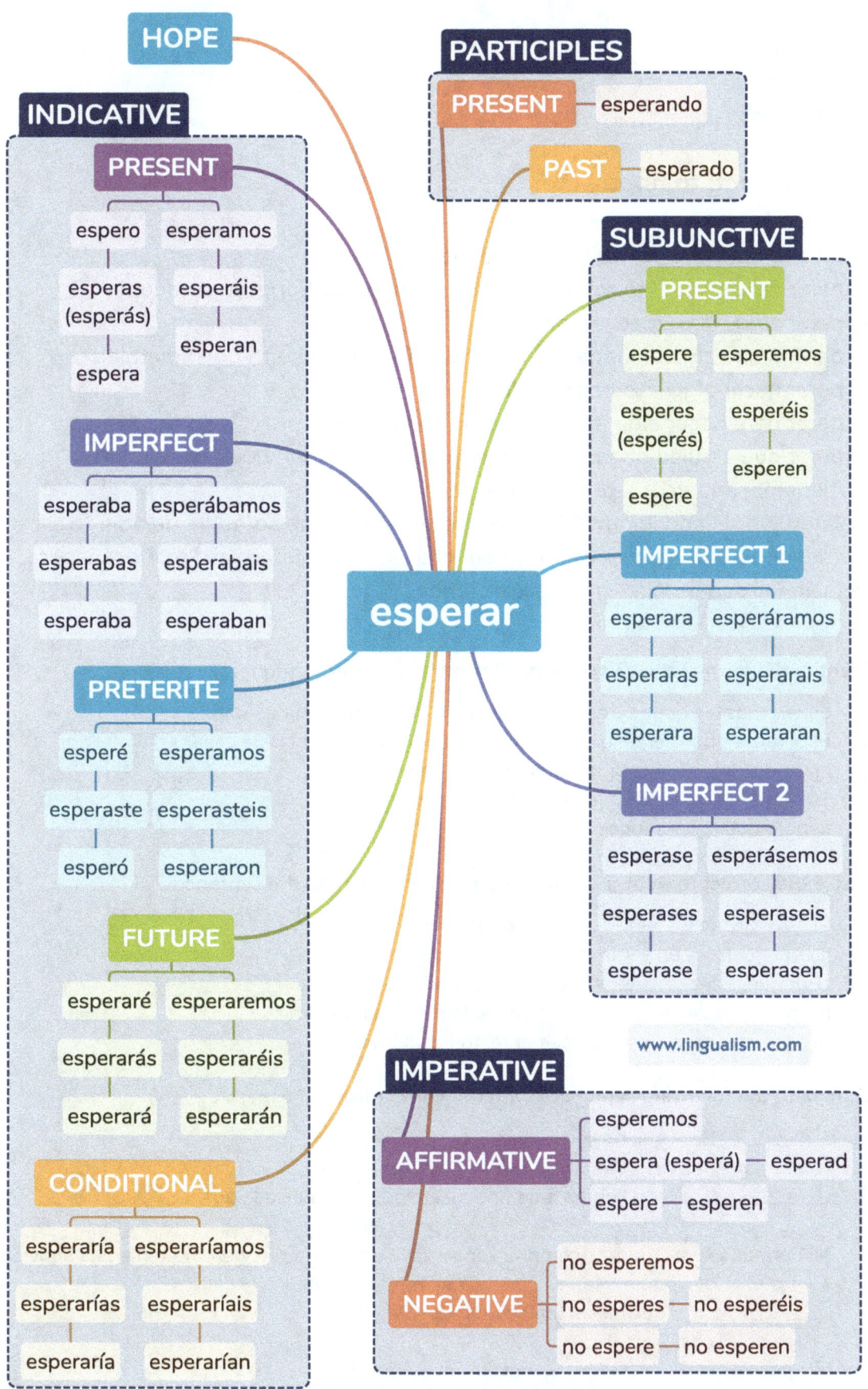

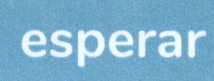

to wait for, expect; to hope
regular -ar verb
- esperar a alguien – to wait for someone
- esperar en alguien – to trust in someone, put one's hopes in someone
- esperar algo – to expect something
- esperar a que alguien haga algo – to wait for someone to do something
- esperar hacer algo – to hope to do something
- esperar para hacer algo – to wait to do something
- esperar que alguien haga algo – to hope that someone does something
- (synonyms) aguardar – to wait for • desear – to wish
- (related words and idioms) ¡Espero que sí/no! – I hope so/not! • de aquí te espero – tremendous, awesome • esperar con interés – to look forward to • desesperar – to dispair • la esperanza – hope, expectation

A. Identify the form of the verb esperar. Then translate the sentences.
1. Esperémoslo a que regrese de vacaciones para contarle la verdad.
2. Esperarás a que llegue el momento adecuado para cambiar de casa.
3. Hace dos años ella estaba esperando un bebé.
4. Siempre espero a mi amigo al salir de clases.
5. Espero que tu idea funcione.

B. Circle the correct form of the verb esperar. Then translate the sentences.
1. Si esperaras/esperemos un poco, podríamos ir juntos.
2. ¡Espera/Espiera un segundo, por favor!
3. ¿Por qué esperas/esperes a que él te llame?
4. No puedo esperar/espero que termine la película para irme.
5. Si esperas/esperaste pacientemente, todo saldrá bien.

C. Complete the following sentences with the correct form of esperar.
1. _____ que no llueva mañana.
   I hope it doesn't rain tomorrow.
2. _____ que llegara a tiempo mi amigo, pero nunca llegó.
   I was hoping my friend would arrive on time, but he never did.
3. Mi hermana y yo _____ comprar ropa nueva en Monterrey, pero no teníamos suficiente dinero.
   My sister and I were hoping to buy new clothes in Monterrey, but we didn't have enough money.
4. _____ que hayas tenido un buen día.
   I hope you had a nice day.
5. Mis jefes no _____ a nadie.
   My bosses don't wait for anyone.

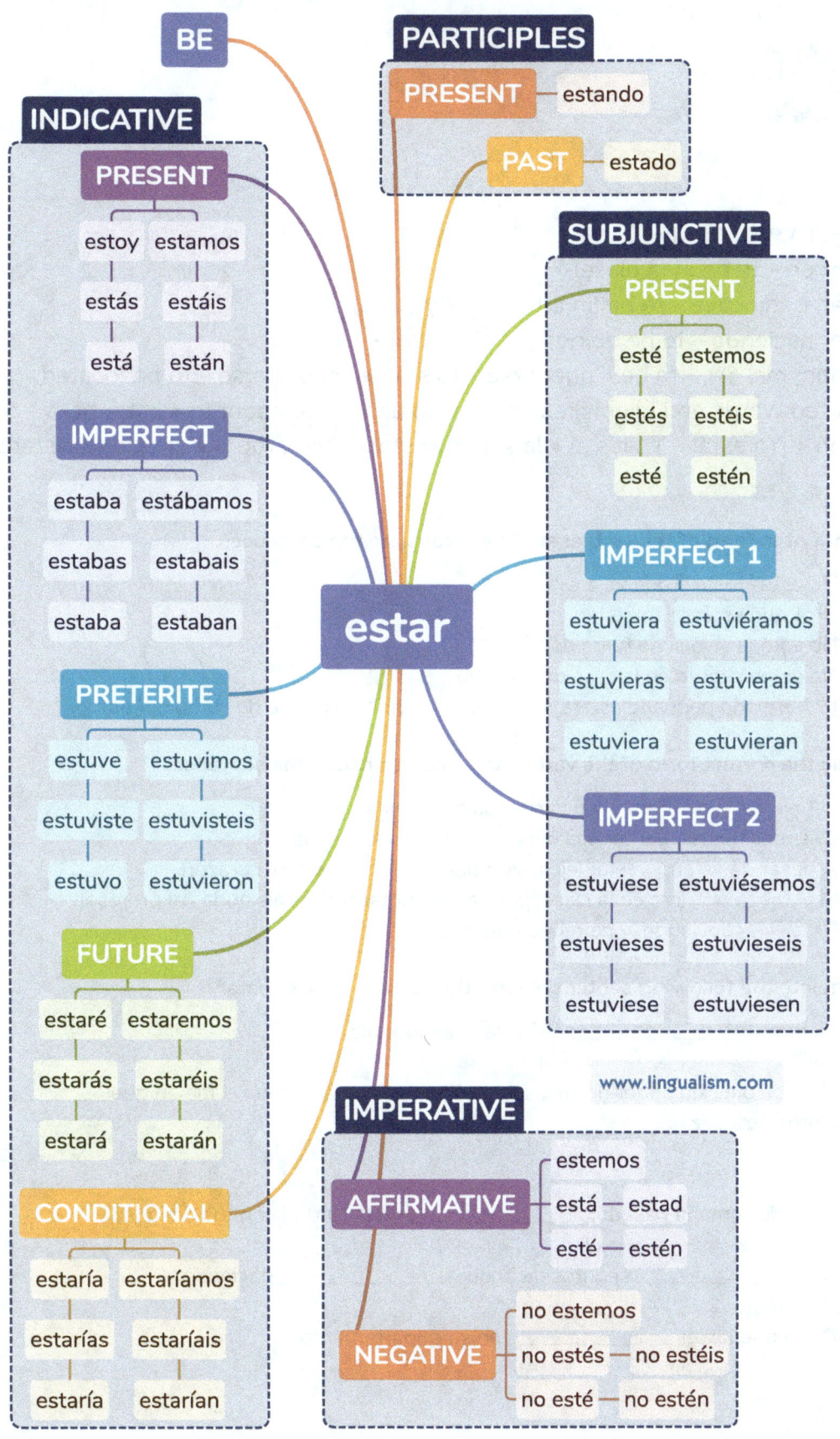

to be

irregular -ar verb: estuv-
- estar en – to be in (a place)
- estar + adjective – to be (in a temporary state)
- estar haciendo – to be doing
- (synonyms) ser – to be • quedarse – to stay • encontrarse – to be located
- (related words and idioms) estar a punto de – to be about to • estar para – to stand for, mean • ¡Ya está! – That's it! • la sala de estar – living room • el estado – state

A. Identify the form of the verb estar. Then translate the sentences.
1. No estés triste. Todo va a estar bien.
2. ¿Por qué estás triste?
3. No estaría vivo si no fuera por ti.
4. No estoy seguro en la casa donde vivo.
5. Mi hermano pequeño estará muy feliz de recibir su regalo de cumpleaños.

B. Circle the correct form of the verb estar. Then translate the sentences.
1. Estuve/Estuvo enfermo y pasé varios días en cama.
2. Después de trabajar todo el día estaba/estuva cansada.
3. A pesar de estando/estar lejos, siempre estés/estás en mi corazón.
4. Si estaba/estuviera en la clase, podría preguntar todas mis dudas al profesor.
5. Está/Estar lloviendo, y no tengo paraguas.

C. Complete the following sentences with the correct form of estar.
1. Siempre _____ aquí para ti, amigo mío.
   I will always be here for you, my friend.
2. Llevaba días sin poder dormir, sabiendo que el sábado sería el día en que _____ juntos otra vez.
   I hadn't been able to sleep for days, knowing that Saturday would be the day we would be together again.
3. El fin de semana pasado, ¿_____ en la ciudad con tus amigos?
   Last weekend, were you in town with your friends?
4. No _____ seguros de lo que _____ haciendo.
   We are not sure what we are doing.
5. Dudo que Javier _____ en su departamento.
   I doubt that Javier is in his apartment.

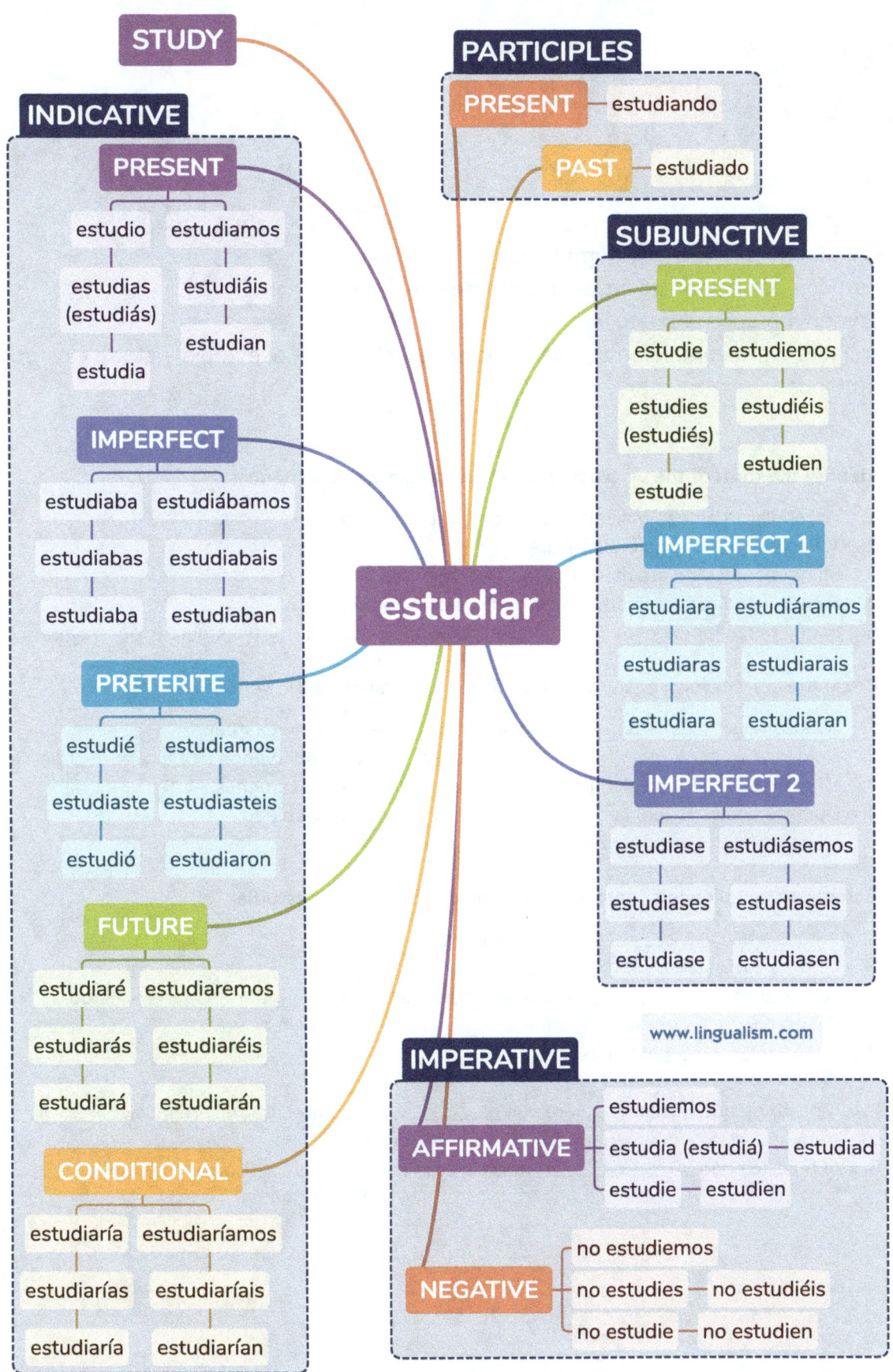

to study
regular -ar verb
- estudiar algo – to study something
- estudiar para algo – to study to become something
- (synonym) aprender – to learn
- (related words and idioms) el/la estudiante – student • el estudio – study • estudioso – studious

A. **Identify the form of the verb estudiar. Then translate the sentences.**
   1. Aprendieron mucho más al estudiar con otro maestro.
   2. A veces estudio en la biblioteca.
   3. Mi hermana estudiará medicina en la UNAM.
   4. Mi hijo estudió alemán en Austria y ahora es bilingüe.
   5. Si quieres tener éxito en la vida, es importante que estudies y te esfuerces por mejorar cada día.

B. **Circle the correct form of the verb estudiar. Then translate the sentences.**
   1. Si Susana estudió/estudiara más, podría aprobar el próximo examen.
   2. Rubí y yo estudiamos/estudiábamos en la biblioteca cuando vimos a una rata en el pasillo.
   3. Mi hermano pequeño siempre estudian/estudia para sus exámenes.
   4. Durante dos años (yo) estudió/estudié español en la universidad.
   5. Mi papá estudiara/estudió ingeniería química.

C. **Complete the following sentences with the correct form of estudiar.**
   1. Vamos a mi casa y _____ juntos.
      Let's go to my house and study together.
   2. Los jóvenes _____ más si no tuvieran que trabajar para pagar sus estudios.
      Young people would study more if they did not have to work to pay for their studies.
   3. ¿_____ para el examen?
      Did you study for the test?
   4. A pesar de que mi mamá quiere que _____ derecho, yo seré músico.
      Even though my mom wants me to study law, I'm going to be a musician.
   5. Al final, los que _____ más salieron con mejores calificaciones.
      In the end, those who studied more came out with better grades.

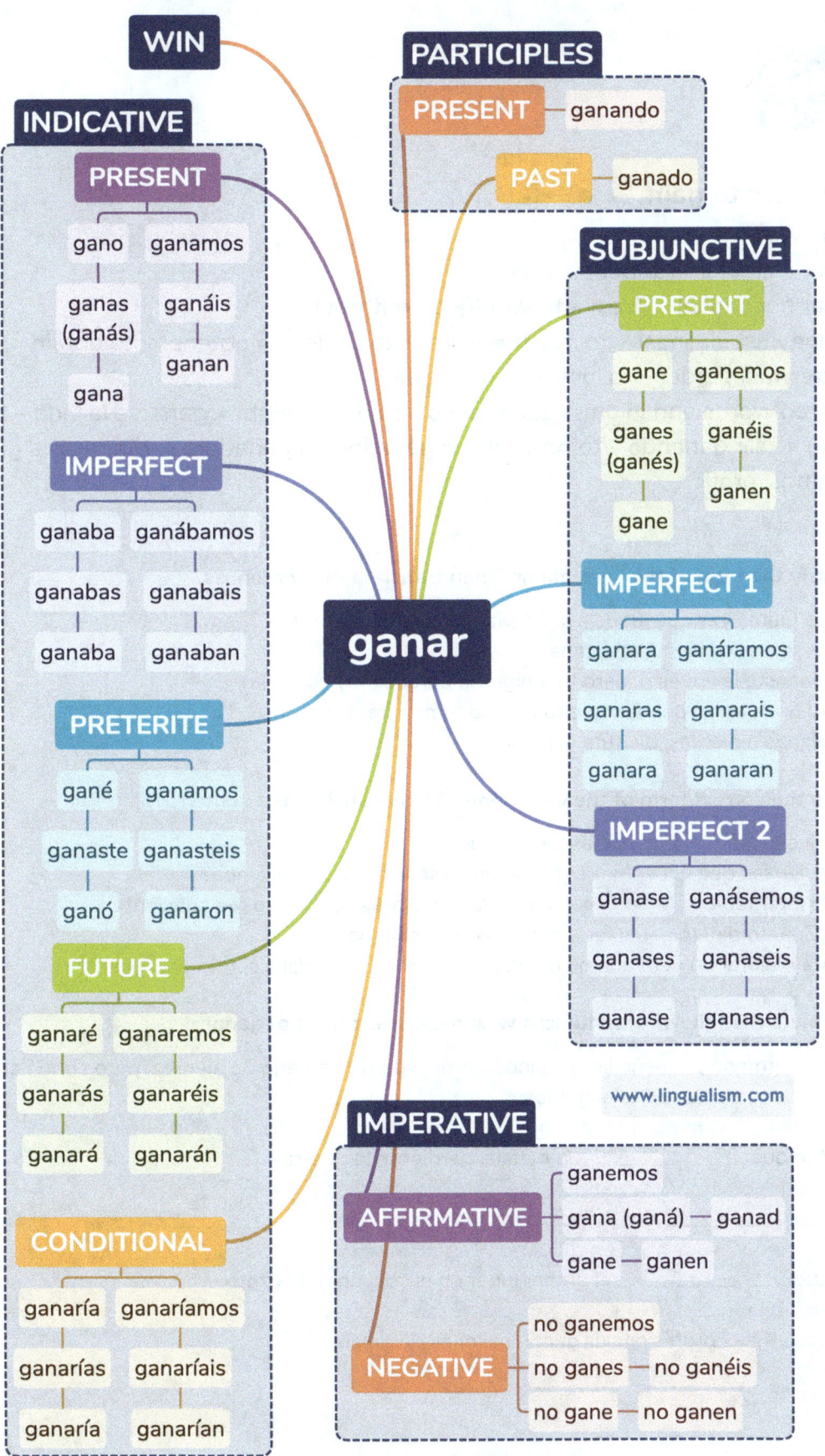

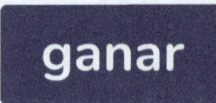

to win; to earn; to gain

regular -ar verb

- ganar a alguien – to beat someone
- ganar por (cinco) a (tres) – to win (five) to (three)
- (synonyms) alcanzar – to reach • lograr – to achieve • obtener – to obtain
- (antonyms) perder – to lose • fallar – to fail
- (related words and idioms) ganar peso – to gain weight • ganarse la vida – to earn a living • salir ganando – to do well • el ganador / la ganadora – winner • la ganancia – earnings, profit

A. Identify the form of the verb ganar. Then translate the sentences.

1. La última vez que jugué a la lotería, gané cinco dólares.
2. Si sigues comiendo así ganarás peso.
3. Ganaste la apuesta, pero tu amigo no parece muy contento.
4. Al final, todos querían que tu equipo terminara ganando.
5. Ganes o pierdas, disfruta el juego.

B. Circle the correct form of the verb ganar. Then translate the sentences.

1. Mi esposo gano/gana más dinero que yo.
2. ¿Piensas que ganan/ganarán a la otra escuela si hacen trampa?
3. Él intentaba gánarse/ganarse la vida como artista, pero no fue suficiente.
4. ¿Cuánto dinero ganaste/ganastes el mes pasado?
5. Va mejorando pero aún no ha ganado/ganando la batalla contra el cáncer.

C. Complete the following sentences with the correct form of ganar.

1. Mi hermano pequeño lloró cuando perdió su primer juego de ajedrez, pero sonrió cuando _____ tres seguidos.
   My little brother cried when he lost his first chess game but smiled when he won three in a row.
2. Aunque _____ la batalla, perdieron la guerra.
   Even though they won the battle, they lost the war.
3. _____ dos juegos, pero ¿podrás seguir _____?
   You won two games, but can you keep winning?
4. Luci _____ el primer lugar en el concurso de canto.
   Luci won first place in the singing contest.
5. Los atletas profesionales ganan millones de dólares.
   Professional athletes earn millions of dollars.

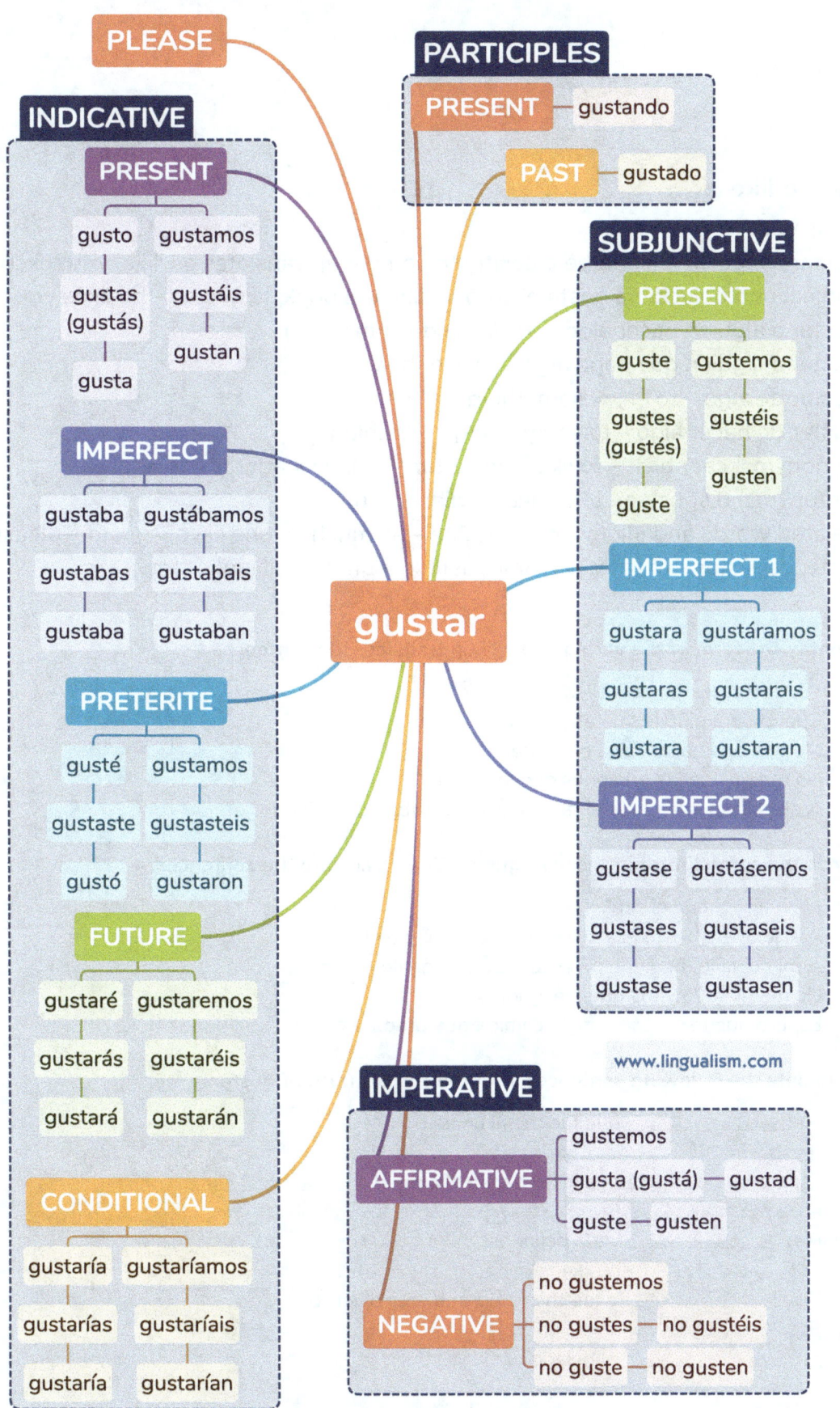

to please; to like
regular -ar verb

- gustar a alguien – (lit. to be pleasing to someone) translates as 'like' with exchange of subject and object: me gusta el libro = I like the book; le gustas – he likes you
- gustar a alguien hacer algo – to like to do something
- gustar a alguien que haga algo – to like that…
- gustar de algo – to enjoy something
- gustar de hacer algo – to enjoy doing something
- (synonyms) caer bien – to like • encantar – to love • adorar – to adore
- (antonyms) disgustar – to dislike • odiar – to hate
- (related words and idioms) como guste – as much as one likes • gusto – pleasure, taste; degustar – to taste, savor • gustoso – gladly, willingly, tasty

A. **Identify the form of the verb gustar. Then translate the sentences.**
1. ¿Qué fruta les gusta a ellos?
2. Cuando era niño le gustaba la pizza.
3. Me gustaría bailar salsa con usted.
4. No me gustan las personas que mienten.
5. A ellas les gusta pasar el rato en el café, hablando y riendo.

B. **Circle the correct form of the verb gustar. Then translate the sentences.**
1. Me gusta/gusto el café.
2. A él le gusta/gustó ella, y a ella le gusta/guste él.
3. A mi novia le gustá/gustó el libro que le regalé.
4. No me gusta/gustas que me ignores.
5. Espero que te gusta/guste la comida que preparé.

C. **Complete the following sentences with the correct form of gustar.**
1. Me _____ que fueras mi novia.
   I would like you to be my girlfriend.
2. Espero que el postre que le preparé a ella pueda _____.
   I hope she might like the dessert I made for her.
3. Me _____ verla bailar así.
   I liked seeing her dance like that.
4. Les _____ a los chicos porque eres divertida.
   Boys like you because you're funny.
5. ¿Te _____ el helado?
   Do you like ice cream?

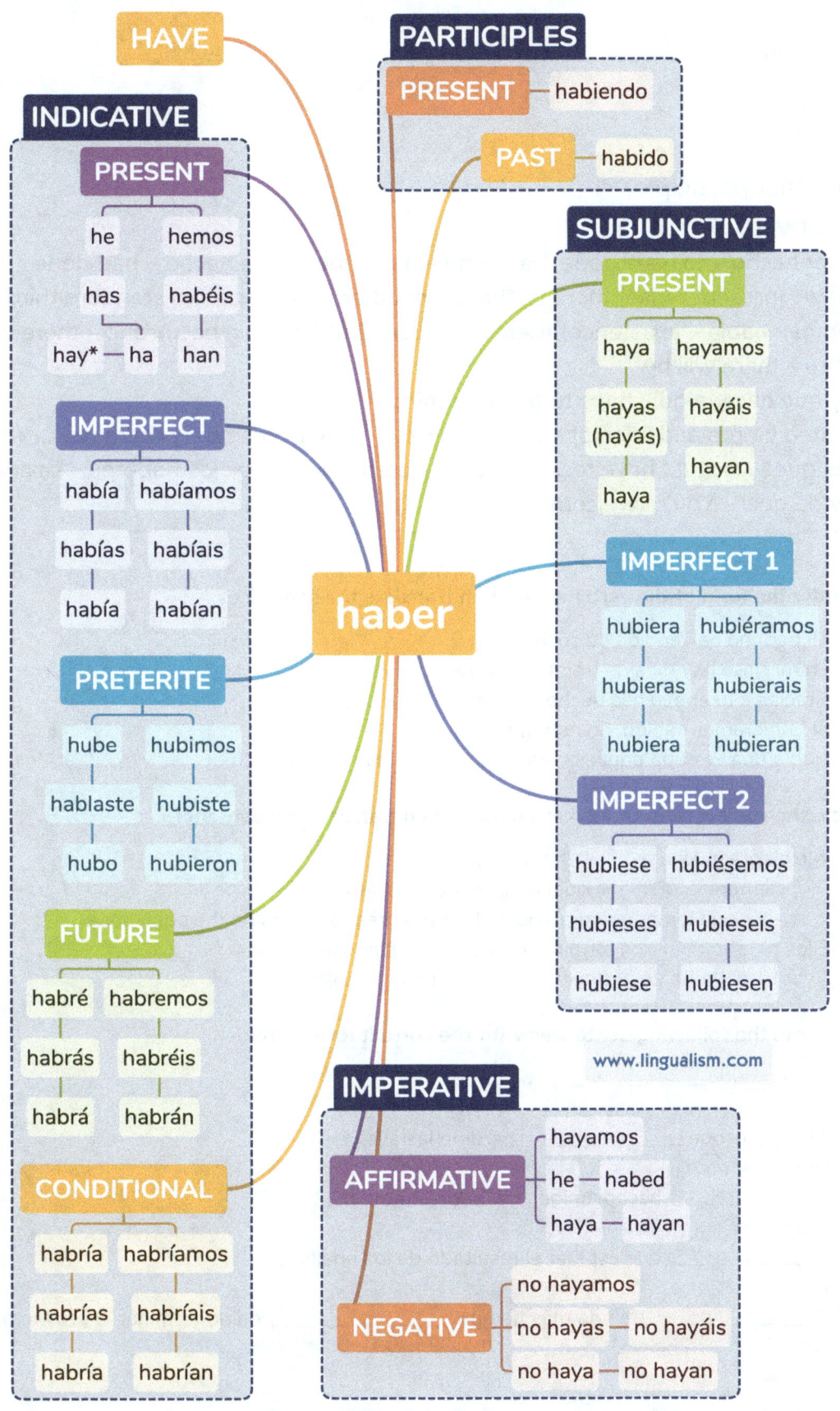

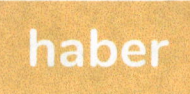

to have (+ past participle)

irregular -er verb

- haber hecho – to have done; ha hecho – has done; había hecho – had done
- * hay – (present tense) there is, there are; other tenses use the standard third-person singular: había – (existence) there was/were; hubo (single occurrence) there was/were; habrá – there will be
- hay que hacer algo – have to do something
- (related words and idioms) había una vez... - once upon a time there was... • no hay más que – you just have to... • el haber – credit, account • los haberes – salary • ¡No hay de qué! – You're welcome!

A. Identify the form of the verb haber. Then translate the sentences.

1. Mi padrino ha vendido su coche.
2. En mi clase hay más de treinta alumnos.
3. Gracias a tu apoyo has hecho una gran diferencia.
4. Si hubiéramos sabido, no habríamos ido.
5. Había una vez una princesa que vivía encerrada en un castillo.

B. Circle the correct form of the verb haber. Then translate the sentences.

1. ¡Me alegra mucho te haber/haberte visto!
2. (Yo) siempre hube/había querido ganar un maratón.
3. He/había que tomar una gran decisión, pero gracias a Dios no me equivoqué.
4. Ellos habrán/hubieron terminado de pintar cuando lleguemos.
5. Ayer había/hubo un accidente en el camino al trabajo.

C. Complete the following sentences with the correct form of haber.

1. ¿Cómo pudo _____ ocurrido?
   How could it have happened?
2. ¡Qué pena que _____ perdido la llave!
   What a shame you lost the key!
3. _____ hecho amigos en todo el mundo.
   We have made friends all over the world.
4. _____ que esperar el resultado de los análisis.
   We will have to wait for the results of the tests.
5. Si _____ tenido más tiempo, _____ podido terminar el proyecto.
   If they had had more time, they would have been able to finish the project.

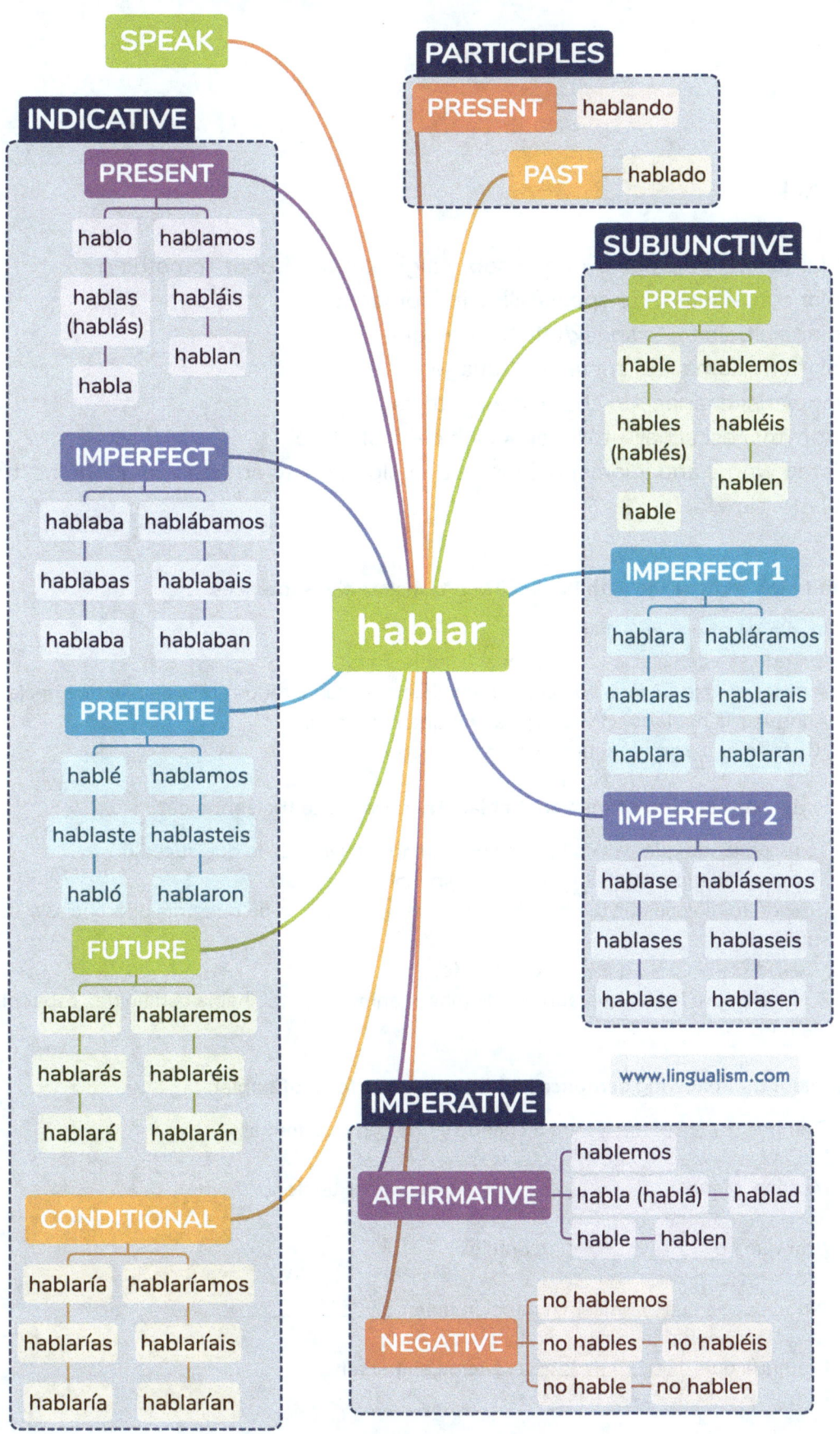

to speak, talk

regular -ar verb

- hablar (acerca) de algo = hablar sobre algo – to talk about something
- hablar con alguien – to speak/talk with someone
- hablar a alguien – to speak/talk to someone
- hablar un idioma – to speak a language
- (synonyms) charlar – to chat • decir – to say
- (antonyms) escuchar – to listen • callar – to shut up
- (related words and idioms) hablar de tú a alguien – to address someone as 'tú' • ¡Ni hablar! – No way!

A. Identify the form of the verb hablar. Then translate the sentences.

1. Juan habla inglés muy bien.
2. Cuando se vean ella le va a hablar a él sobre su futuro.
3. A pesar de que Diviana hablara con un acento extraño, todos entendían lo que decía.
4. Aunque ella hablaba en voz baja, se notaba enfadada.
5. ¿Cuándo hablaste por última vez con tu madre?

B. Circle the correct form of the verb hablar. Then translate the sentences.

1. Te recomiendo que hables/hablas con tu madre acerca de lo que sucedió.
2. Mi madre siempre me hablo/habla en español.
3. Cuando fuimos novios también hablábamos/hablabamos de nuestras diferencias y cómo superarlas.
4. ¿Cuándo hablaraste/hablarás con tu jefe?
5. A ella siempre le han gustado los idiomas, y ahora habla/se habla con fluidez español, francés y alemán.

C. Complete the following sentences with the correct form of hablar.

1. Siempre _____ de ti cuando estoy con mis amigas.
   I always talk about you when I'm with my friends.
2. Mañana, María _____ con su amiga por teléfono.
   Tomorrow, María will talk to her friend on the phone.
3. ¿Por qué no _____ conmigo?
   Why aren't you talking to me?
4. ¡No _____ más! Yo también quiero _____.
   Don't talk anymore! I want to talk, too.
5. Preferiría que _____ ese tema en persona.
   I'd rather we talk about it in person.

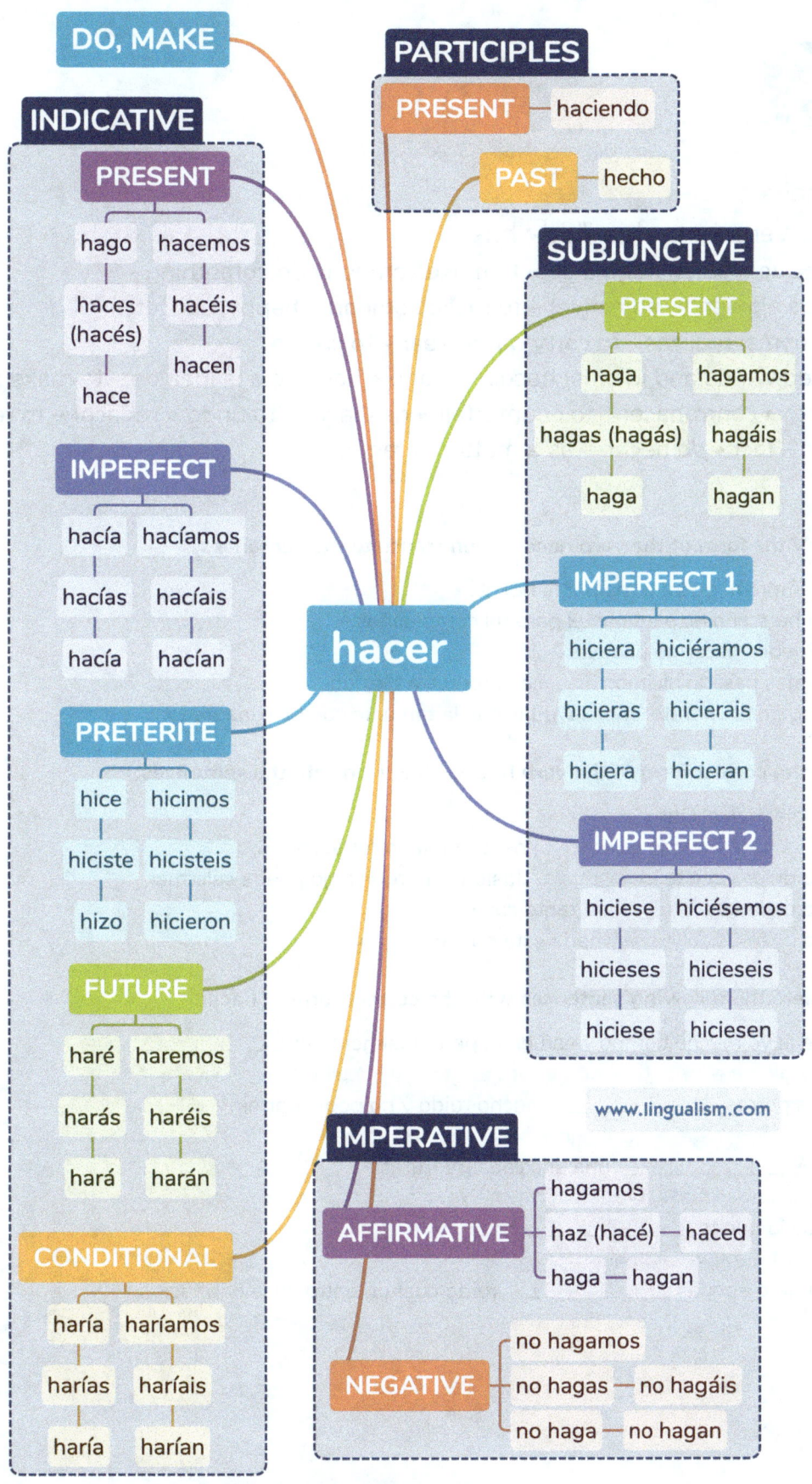

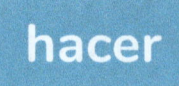

to do; to make

irregular -er verb: hag-, hiz-/hic-; ha-
- hacer que alguien haga algo – to make someone do something
- hacer a alguien (+ adjective) – to make someone (happy, sad, etc.)
- (synonyms) realizar – to carry out • crear – to create
- (related words and idioms) hace… - … ago • hacerse a la idea de – to make up one's mind to • contrahacer – to counterfeit • deshacer – to undo • rehacer – to redo • el hecho – fact • de hecho – as a matter of fact

A. Identify the form of the verb hacer. Then translate the sentences.
1. Siempre hago mi tarea por la noche.
2. Mi hermano hizo un pastel para mi cumpleaños.
3. ¿Puedes hacerme un favor?
4. El mes pasado hicimos un viaje sorpresa a México.
5. Hagamos un trato: si me ayudas con la tarea, te compro una pizza.

B. Circle the correct form of the verb hacer. Then translate the sentences.
1. ¿Hola, Paula! Qué haces/hices?
2. Hizo/Hacía mucho calor y (yo) necesitaba un refresco frío.
3. No quiero que te hagas/hayas ilusiones porque algo puede salir mal.
4. No creía que hará/hiciera tanto calor.
5. No hazamos/hagamos nada esta noche.

C. Complete the following sentences with the correct form of hacer.
1. Me llevó mucho tiempo y esfuerzo, pero finalmente lo _____.
   It took me a lot of time and effort, but finally I finished the thesis.
2. Los perros _____ mucho ruido y no podía dormir.
   The dogs made a lot of noise, and I couldn't sleep.
3. Hoy _____ una ensalada de frutas.
   Today I will make a fruit salad.
4. Haz lo que te _____ feliz.
   Do what makes you happy.
5. Mi gato apenas _____ ruido cuando entró en la habitación.
   My cat barely made a sound when he entered the room.

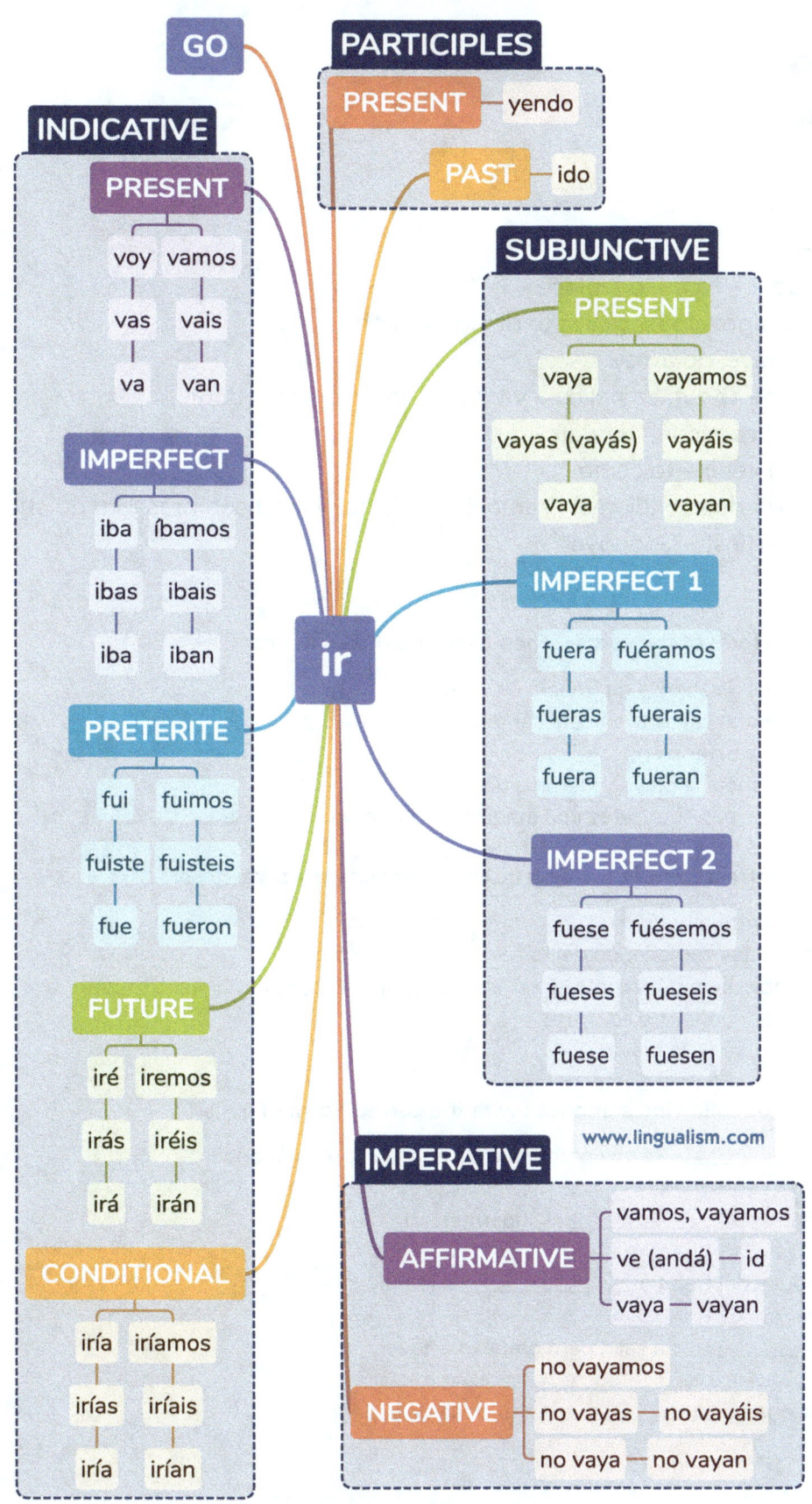

ir

to go

regular -ir verb

- ir a un lugar – to go to a place
- ir a hacer algo – to be going to do something
- irse – to leave, go away
- ir de – to be about: La película va de… - The movie is about…
- (synonym) caminar – to walk
- (antonym) venir – to come
- (related words and idioms) ¡Vamos! – Let's go! • ir de compras – to go shopping • ¡Vaya con Díos! – Goodbye!

A. **Identify the form of the verb ir. Then translate the sentences.**

1. Todos los días voy a mi trabajo en autobús.
2. Prefiero que vayas a la fiesta con ella.
3. Todo va a estar bien.
4. Ayer fueron a la playa y vieron a un delfín.
5. ¿A dónde irías si tuvieras una máquina del tiempo?

B. **Circle the correct form of the verb ir. Then translate the sentences.**

1. Me encontré a tu tío cuando iba/fue para tu casa.
2. Si continúas cometiendo delitos irás/vayas a la cárcel.
3. Él siempre la miraba como si fuera/era a decirle algo, pero nunca lo hacía.
4. ¿A dónde fue/vio usted?
5. Ellos ven/van a la playa.

C. **Complete the following sentences with the correct form of ir.**

1. ¿_____ a comprar una casa nueva el próximo año?
   Are you going to buy a new house next year?
2. El martes _____ al supermercado.
   On Tuesday I went to the supermarket.
3. Después del trabajo _____ a la playa.
   After work we go to the beach.
4. _____ a salir, pero empezó a llover.
   We were going to go out, but it started to rain.
5. ¿Por qué no _____ a tu clase de español?
   Why didn't you go to your Spanish class?

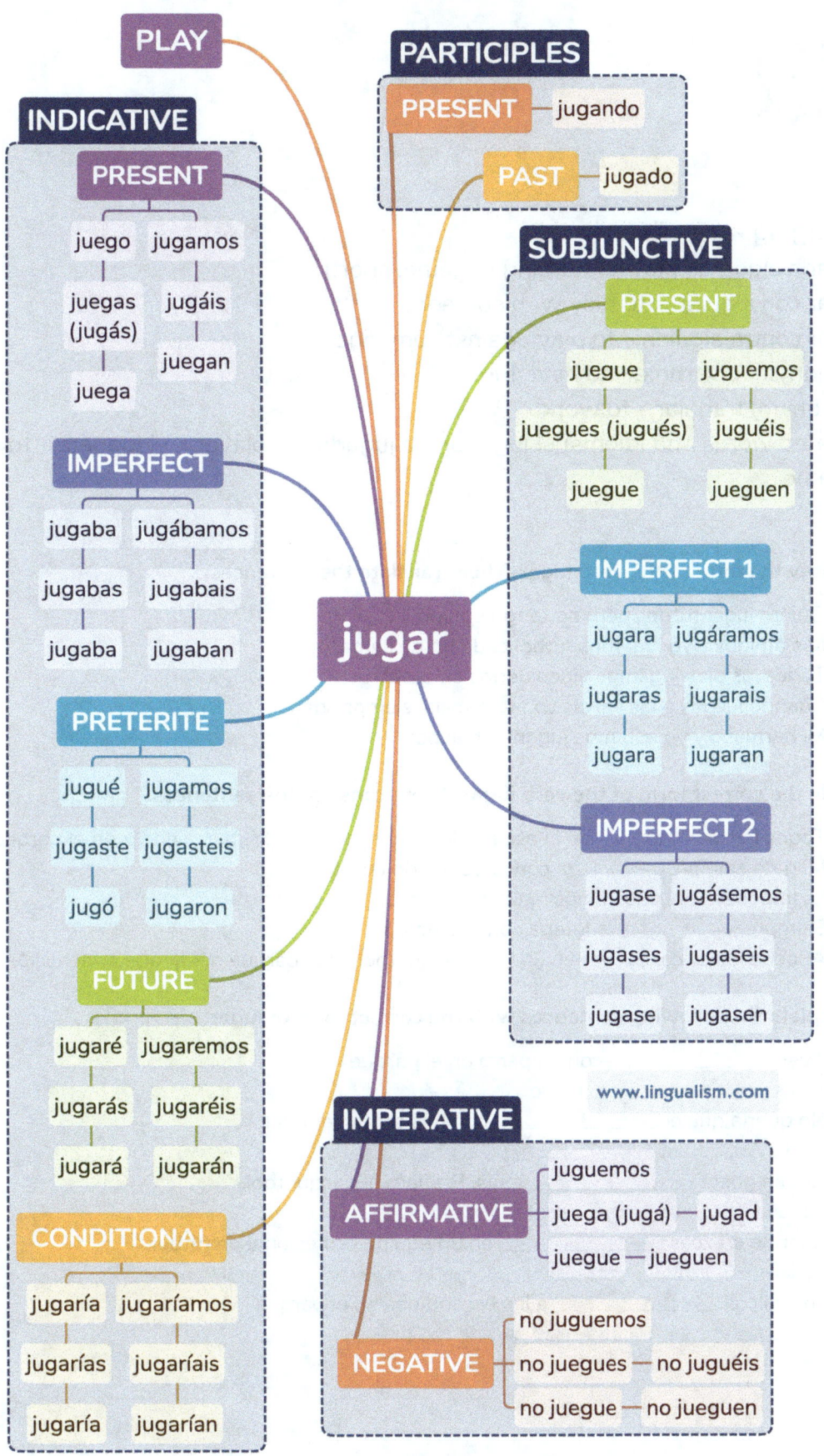

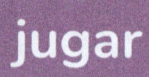

jugar

to play

stem-changing -ar verb: u → ue
- jugar a algo – to play something (a game, sport)
- jugar con alguien – to play with someone
- jugar contra alguien – to play against someone
- (synonym) divertirse – to have fun
- (antonym) trabajar – to work
- (related words and idioms) el jugador / la jugadora – player • el juguete – toy • el juego – game

A. **Identify the form of the verb jugar. Then translate the sentences.**
1. Quiero jugar fútbol, pero no tengo equipo.
2. Mis amigos y yo jugamos fútbol cada fin de semana.
3. Todos los días jugamos videojuegos en casa.
4. Cuando juegas a las cartas con tu familia, siempre ganas.
5. Mi hermano y yo estamos jugando béisbol.

B. **Circle the correct form of the verb jugar. Then translate the sentences.**
1. Todos los días después de la escuela los niños jugaron/jugaban ajedrez en el parque.
2. Mi gato siempre juega/jiega con la pelota de tenis.
3. Es importante que los niños juguen/jueguen.
4. Siempre juego/jugo a la lotería con mis tíos.
5. Anoche los chicos jugaron/juegaron basquetbol en el parque hasta que anocheció.

C. **Complete the following sentences with the correct form of jugar.**
1. Ayer _____ con mi perro en el parque.
   Yesterday I played with my dog in the park.
2. No quería que él _____ con mis sentimientos.
   I didn't want him to play with my feelings.
3. No me gusta _____ tenis. Prefiero el básquetbol.
   I don't like to play tennis. I prefer basketball.
4. Cuando crezcas _____ en un equipo profesional de fútbol.
   When you grow up, you will play in a professional soccer team.
5. Los chicos _____ a las escondidas en el parque.
   The boys are playing hide and seek in the park.

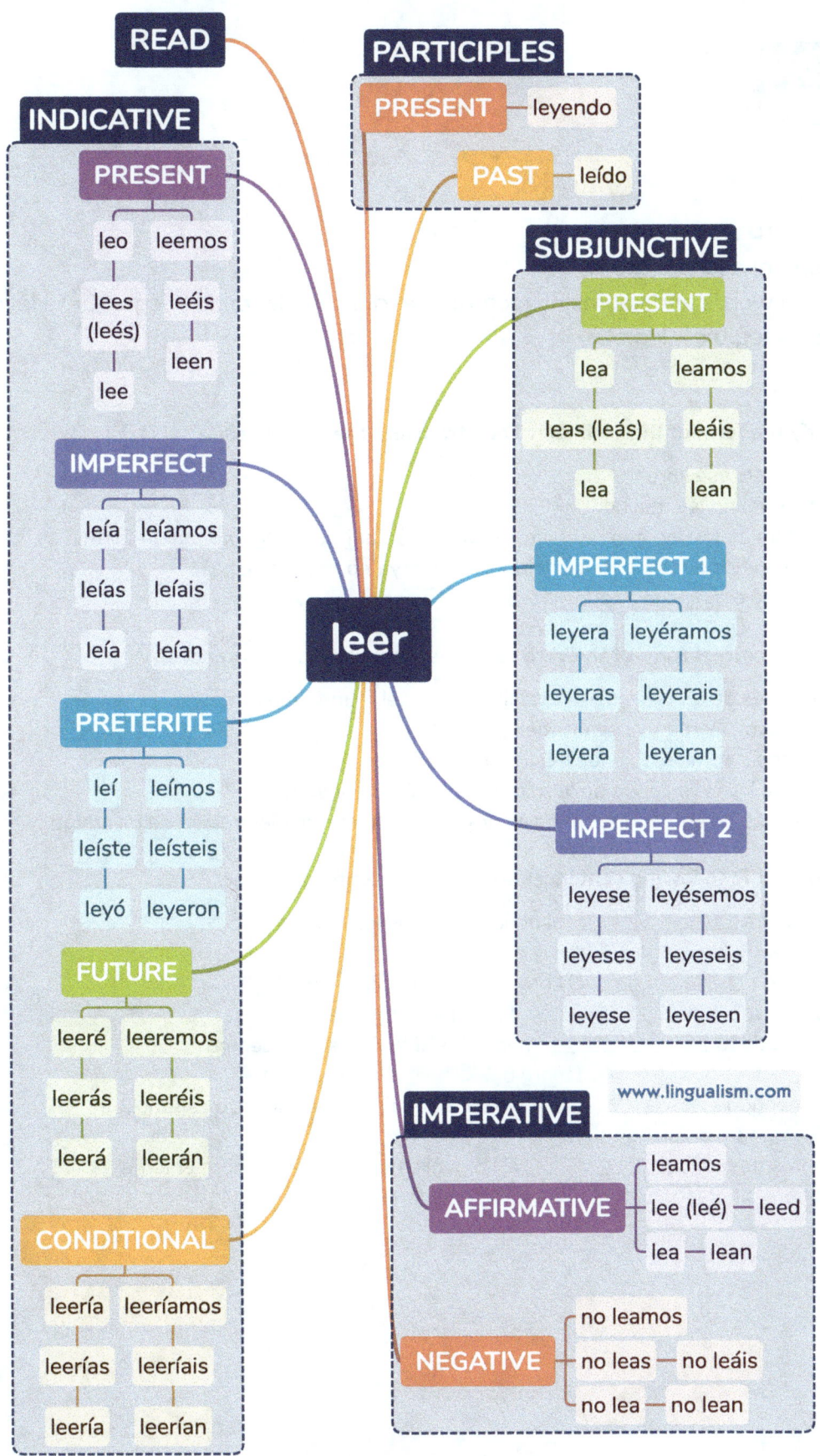

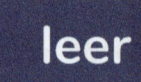

leer

to read

regular -er verb

- (antonym) escribir – to write
- (related words and idioms) la lectura – reading • la leyenda – legend • la lección – lesson • legible – legible

A. **Identify the form of the verb leer. Then translate the sentences.**
   1. ¿Ya leíste ese libro?
   2. Mi hermano lee mucho.
   3. Generalmente leo muchas historias de terror, aunque luego no pueda dormir.
   4. Hace varios años (yo) había leído ese libro, ya no me acordaba.
   5. Cuando era niño leía todos los días.

B. **Circle the correct form of the verb leer. Then translate the sentences.**
   1. Después de que leas/leyes este libro, verás el mundo diferente.
   2. Por favor, léeme/me lée un cuento.
   3. Ambos leeron/leyeron los tres libros en un mes.
   4. Estaba leíndo/leyendo un libro de terror cuando oí un ruido.
   5. Después de años sin saber de él, hoy leí/leyí un correo electrónico de mi amigo.

C. **Complete the following sentences with the correct form of leer.**
   1. Mi padre _____ el periódico todos los días.
      My father reads the newspaper every day.
   2. Ella no _____ el libro si no le gusta la trama.
      She won't read the book if she doesn't like the plot.
   3. Sin duda tú _____ más libros si tuvieras más tiempo.
      No doubt you would read more books if you had more time.
   4. A menudo _____ en voz alta para practicar nuestro español.
      We often read aloud to practice our Spanish.
   5. Antes de que _____ el libro, ella no sabía nada sobre el tema.
      Before she read the book, she knew nothing about it.

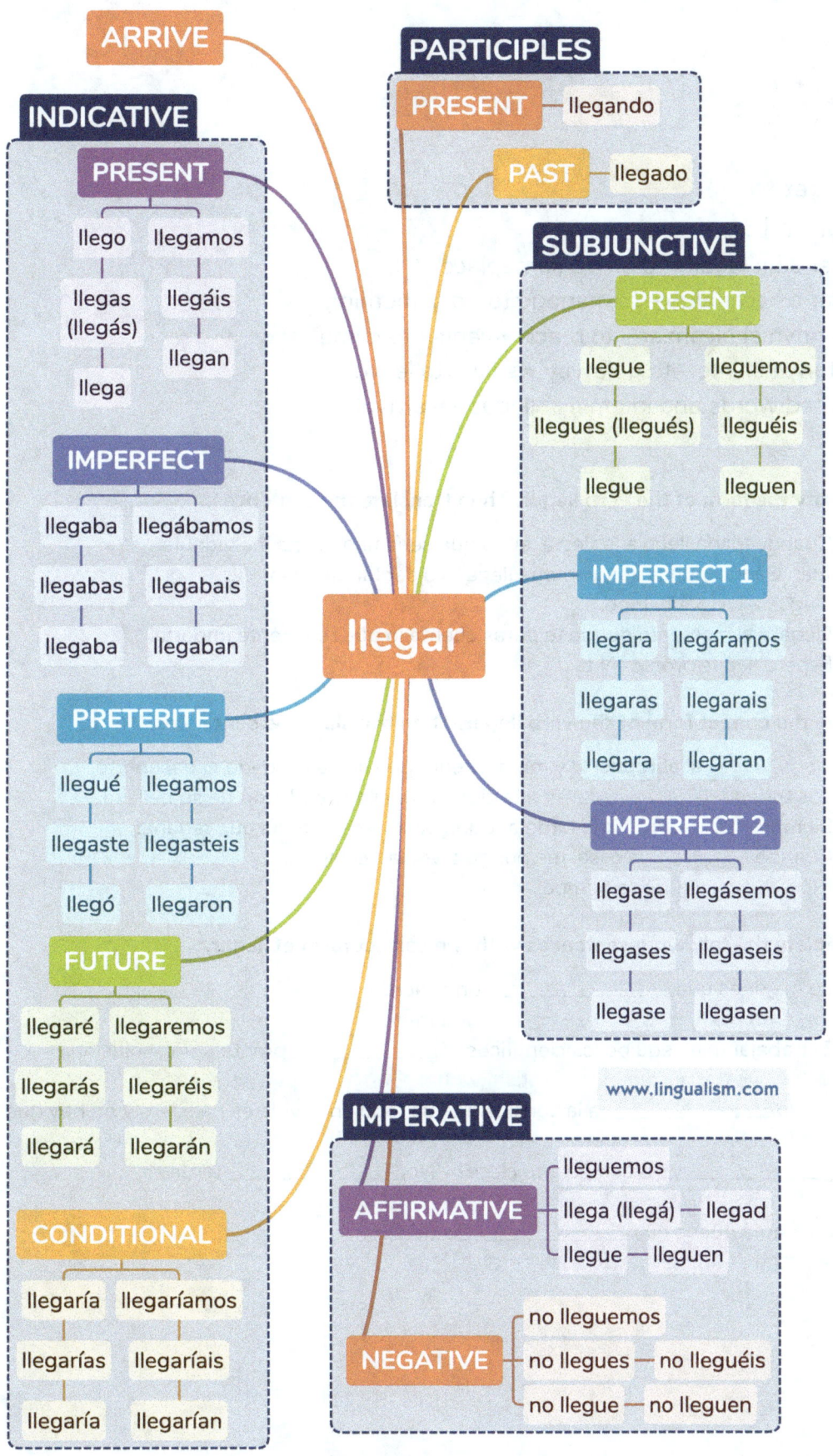

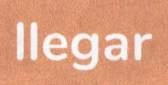

llegar

to arrive, get to

regular -ar verb; g → gu

- llegar a un lugar – to arrive someplace
- llegar a hacer algo – to manage to do something
- (synonyms) alcanzar – to reach • venir – to come
- (antonyms) irse – to go away • salir – to leave
- (related words and idioms) la llegada – arrival

A. **Identify the form of the verb llegar. Then translate the sentences.**

1. Cuando María llegó a la fiesta, supo que sería una noche inolvidable.
2. Juan Gabriel nunca imaginó que llegaría a ser tan famoso.
3. Llegaste justo a tiempo.
4. Llegará el momento donde te darás cuenta lo que realmente importa.
5. Espero llegue pronto mi taxi.

B. **Circle the correct form of the verb llegar. Then translate the sentences.**

1. Llegué/Llegé al aeropuerto y me di cuenta que había olvidado el pasaporte.
2. Los turistas llegaban/llegaron a la ciudad y se sorprendieron de su belleza.
3. Siempre llegabas/lleguías tarde al trabajo y tu jefe te tenía que regañar.
4. Cuando llego/lliego a casa, me pongo a ver la televisión.
5. ¡No llegarás/llegarés a tiempo!

C. **Complete the following sentences with the correct form of llegar.**

1. Lo mejor es que _____ a un acuerdo.
   The best thing is that we reach an agreement.
2. Si trabajaran en equipo los científicos _____ pronto a una solución.
   If they worked as a team, scientists would soon arrive at a solution.
3. Pablo _____ a la conclusión que todo en la vida es pasajero y no hay que preocuparse.
   Pablo came to the conclusion that everything in life is temporary and there is no need to worry.
4. ¿_____ a tiempo a tu clase? - No, _____ tarde.
   Did you get to your class on time? – No, I'm late.
5. Mi mamá quería que _____ a tiempo.
   My mom wanted you to be on time.

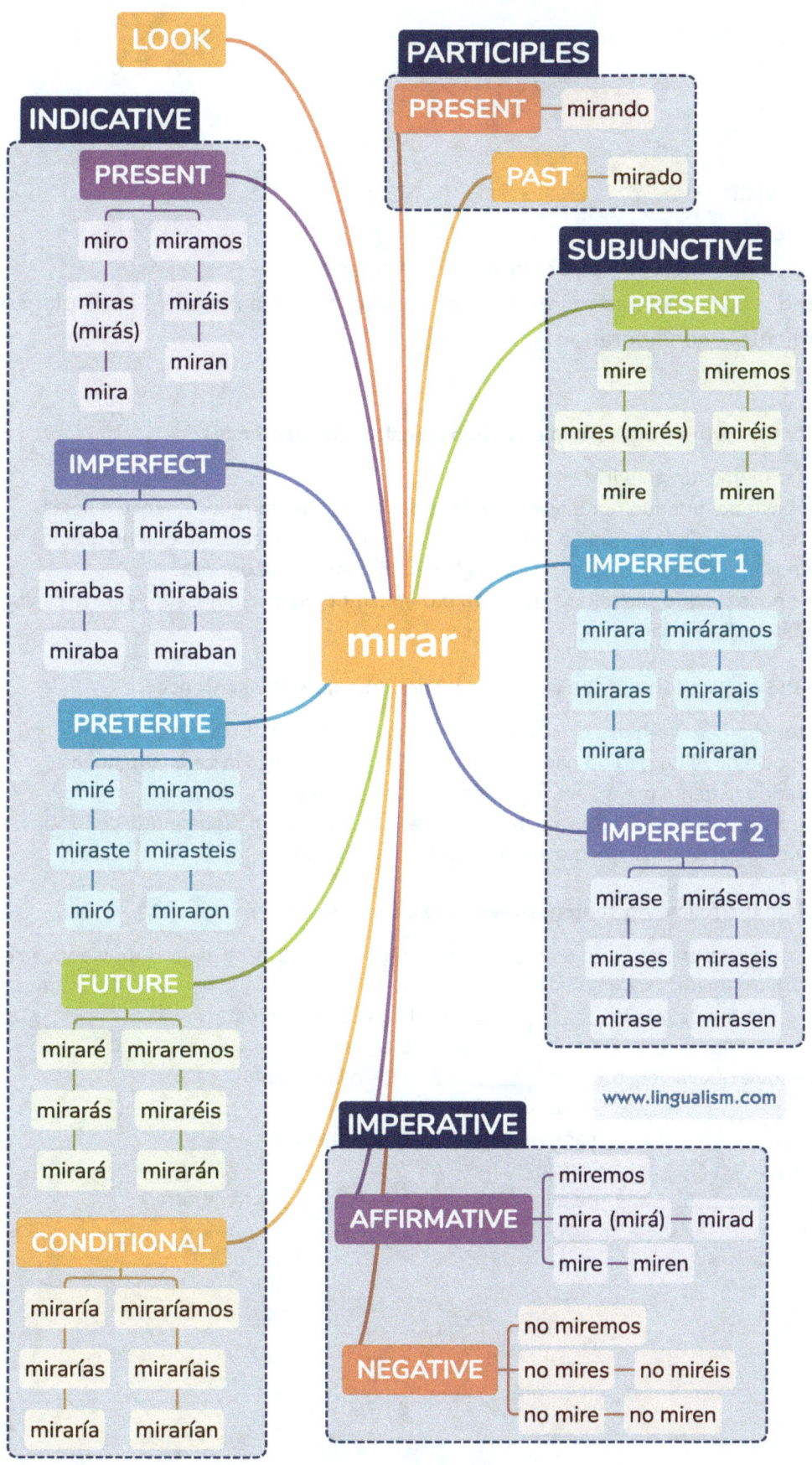

mirar

to look at, watch
regular -ar verb
- (synonyms) observar – to observe • ver – to see
- (related words and idioms) el mirador – viewpoint • la mirada – look, glance • el miramiento – consideration

A. Identify the form of the verb mirar. Then translate the sentences.
1. ¡Mira mamá, un arco iris!
2. Ella estaba mirando por la ventana, cuando se dió cuenta que comenzó a llover.
3. Axel siempre miraba por la ventana cuando tenía que hacer algo que no quería.
4. Si miras el mapa con detenimiento, ¿Cuántos edificios reconoces?
5. Después de que ella mirara su aspecto demacrado en el espejo, supo que necesitaba cambiar sus hábitos alimenticios.

B. Circle the correct form of the verb mirar. Then translate the sentences.
1. Raquel miró/miro hacia el cielo y estaba lleno de estrellas brillantes.
2. Todavía no te he pedido nada, salvo que me miras/mires a la cara y no huyas.
3. Cuando la gente me miran/mira, siento que me están juzgando.
4. Karen estaba mirando/miraba por la ventana cuando pasó alguien que conocía.
5. Él la miría/miraba fijamente, pero ella no le hacía caso.

C. Complete the following sentences with the correct form of mirar.
1. A través del cristal _____ al animalito mientras se alejaba moviendo la cabeza.
   Through the glass, I watched the little animal as he walked away shaking his head.
2. A veces me da miedo _____ a la gente a los ojos.
   Sometimes it scares me to look people in the eye.
3. Siempre que la veo, me _____ a los ojos y sonríe.
   Whenever I see her, she looks me in the eye and smiles.
4. Él la _____ fijamente mientras ella le hablaba.
   He stared at her as she spoke to him.
5. _____ un tigre a los ojos es _____ a la muerte.
   To look a tiger in the eye is to look at death.

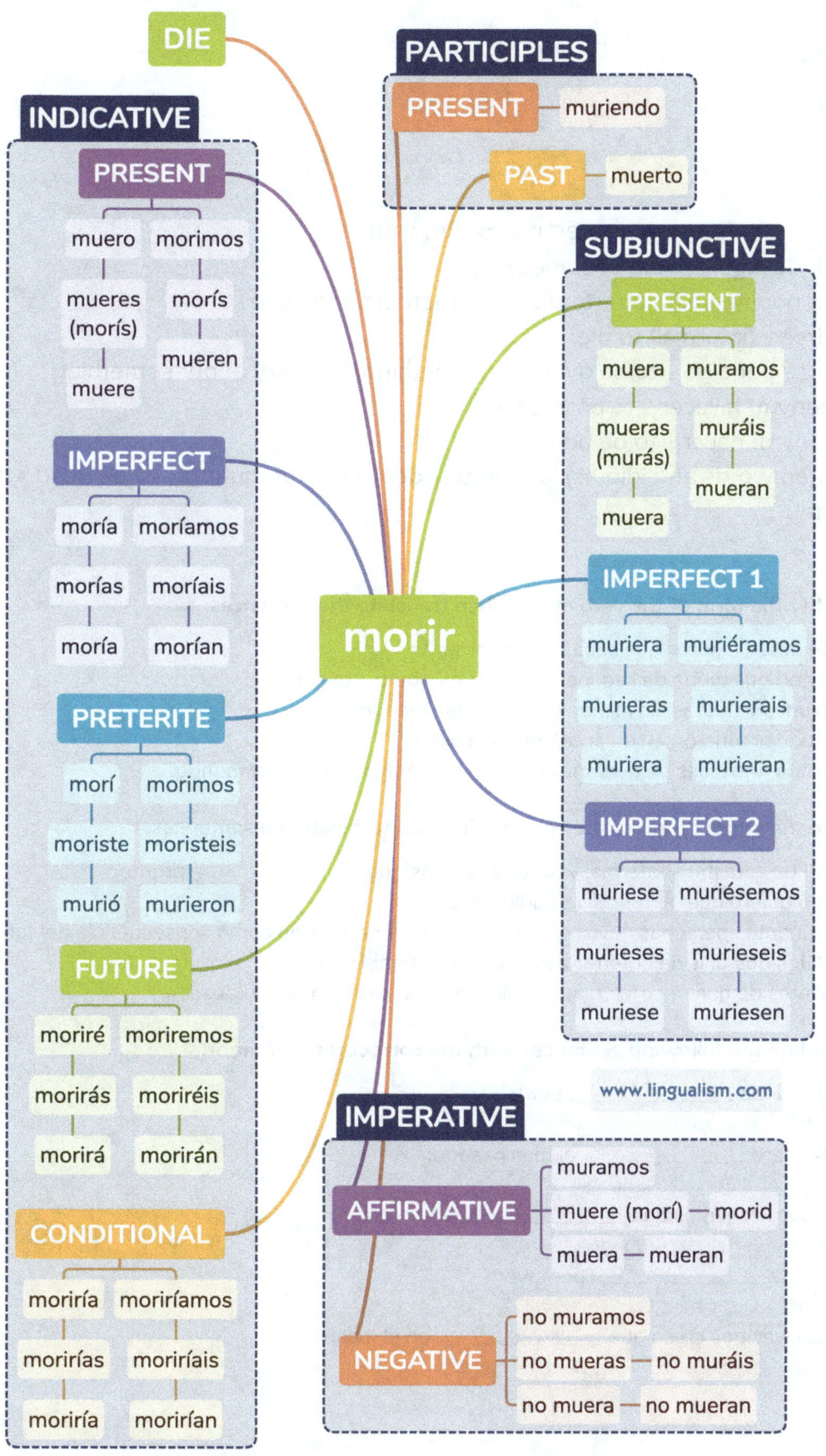

to die

irregular stem-changing -ir verb: o → ue; mur-
- morir de algo – to die of something
- morir por algo/alguien – to die for something/someone
- morirse – (informal) to die
- morirse por algo – to be dying for something, be crazy about something
- (synonym) fallecer – to pass away
- (antonym) nacer – to be born
- (related words and idioms) la muerte – death • estar muerto – to be dead • mortal – mortal

A. Identify the form of the verb morir. Then translate the sentences.
1. Si muero, quiero que sepas que te amé.
2. Sentí que moría de sed, pero el agua estaba contaminada.
3. Nunca te rindas sin luchar, o morirás arrepentido.
4. Todos murieron en un accidente de coche.
5. Cada año miles de personas mueren de hambre en todo el mundo.

B. Circle the correct form of the verb morir. Then translate the sentences.
1. Mi tía está muy enferma, y todos sabemos que va a morir/morirá pronto.
2. No quiero que mura/muera nadie más.
3. ¿Cuántas personas mueren/mueran al mes en el mundo como consecuencia del tabaco?
4. A los dos días de enterrar a su esposa, él también murió/morió.
5. Antes de que muera/muriera doña Gregoria pidió un último deseo.

C. Complete the following sentences with the correct form of morir.
1. Sin duda _____ por ti.
   She would surely die for you.
2. Mi gato _____ el mes pasado.
   My cat died last month.
3. Todos tenemos que _____ algún día.
   We must all die someday.
4. ¡No te _____, por favor!
   Don't die, please!
5. Los vecinos creen que _____ en el incendio.
   The neighbors think we died in the fire.

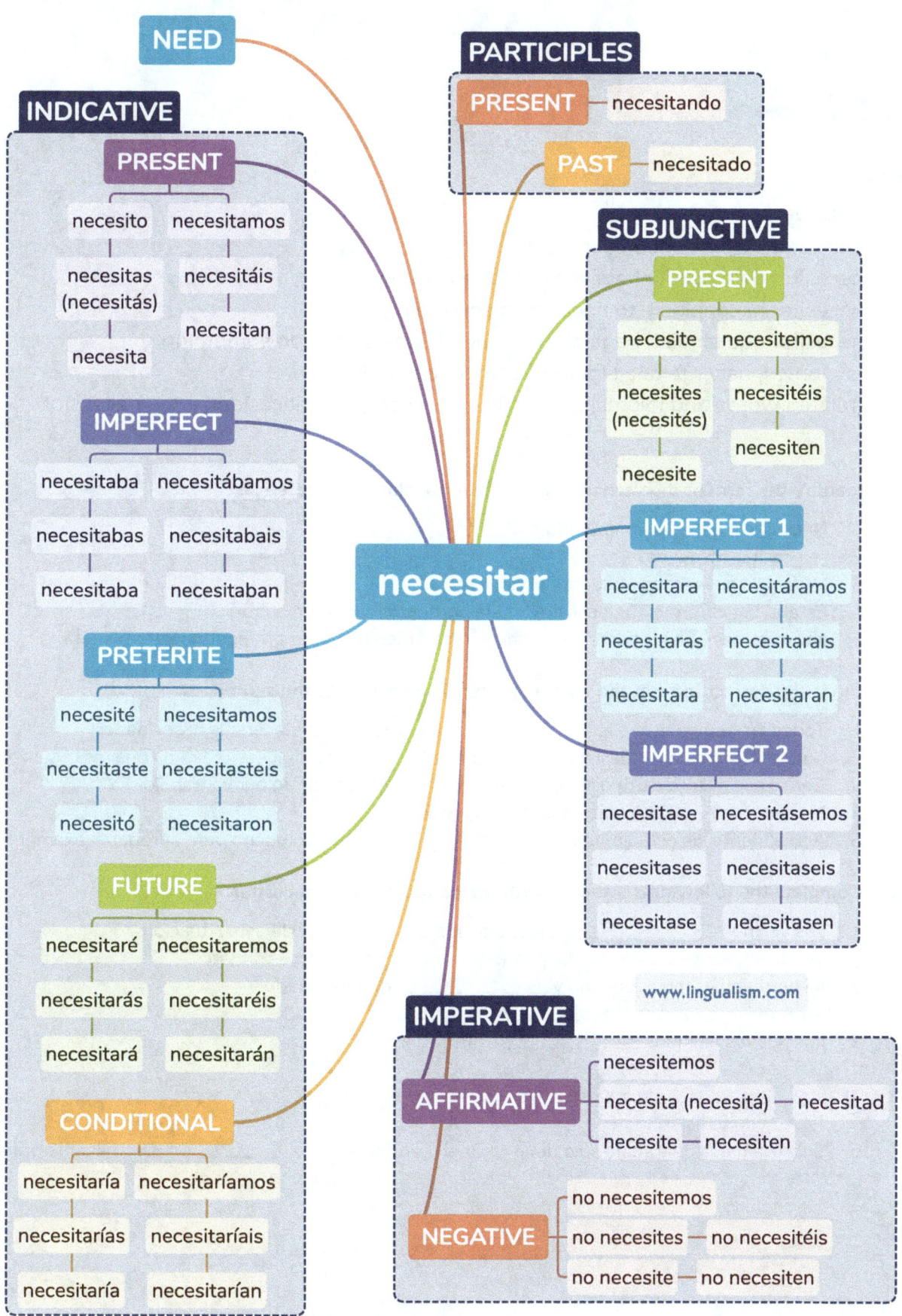

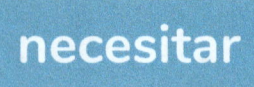

to need

regular -ar verb
- necesitar algo – to need something
- necesitar de algo – to have a need for something
- necesitar hacer algo – to need to do something
- necesitar que alguien haga algo – to need someone to do something
- (synonym) hacer falta a alguien – someone needs
- (related words and idioms) necesario – necessary • la necesidad – the necessity

A. **Identify the form of the verb necesitar. Then translate the sentences.**
1. Necesito una nueva computadora.
2. ¿Necesitas mi ayuda?
3. Mi familia necesitaba un lugar donde vivir.
4. Estaba tan enfermo que necesité ayuda para terminar el proyecto.
5. Necesitamos que los líderes mundiales tomen medidas para proteger nuestro planeta.

B. **Circle the correct form of the verb necesitar. Then translate the sentences.**
1. Todas las personas necesitan/necesitamos dinero para satisfacer sus necesidades.
2. Cuando vivimos en el desierto constantemente necesitaban/necesitábamos nuevas provisiones.
3. Con el nacimiento de tu hijo necesitará/necesitas encontrar un nuevo trabajo.
4. No necesito/necesieto más de lo que ya tengo.
5. Actualmente los estudiantes necesitan/se necesita estudiar mucho para aprobar el examen.

C. **Complete the following sentences with the correct form of necesitar.**
1. Los vecinos _____ nuestra ayuda si quieren salir de esta situación.
   The neighbors will need our help if they want to get out of this situation.
2. Mi hermano es muy pequeño y _____ de mi cuidado.
   My brother is very little, and he needs my care.
3. Los nuevos alumnos _____ nuestra ayuda.
   The new students will need our help.
4. _____ que me escuches.
   I need you to listen to me.
5. Sobre la mesa de trabajo solo debe estar el material que _____ para hacer la práctica.
   Only the material you need to do the practice should be on the worktable.

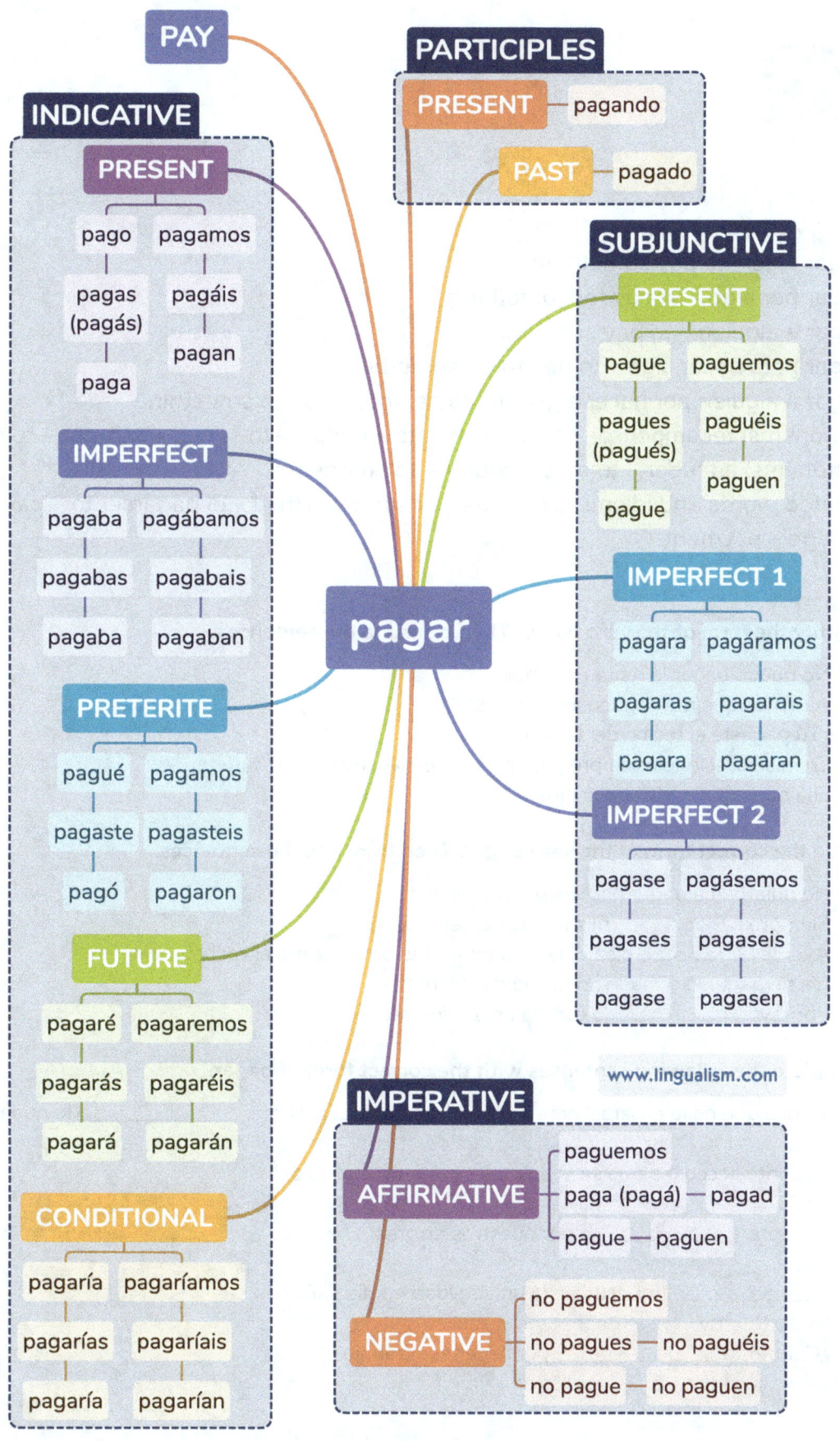

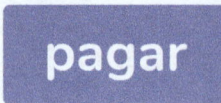

pagar

to pay

regular -ar verb; g → gu

- pagar algo – to pay something
- pagar por algo – to pay for something
- pagar a alguien – to pay someone
- pagar para hacer algo – to pay to do something
- pagar a alguien por hacer algo – to pay someone to do something
- (synonyms) recompensar – to compensate • gastar – to spend • tributar – to pay taxes
- (antonyms) adeudar – to owe • cobrar – to charge for
- (related words and idioms) ¡No paga! – It's not worth it! • el pagamento – pay, salary • el pago – payment

A. **Identify the form of the verb pagar. Then translate the sentences.**

1. No puedo pagar la renta este mes.
2. A menos que me paguen, no lo haré.
3. ¿Tú pagaste el recibo del teléfono?
4. En mis vacaciones siempre pagaba en efectivo, nunca con tarjeta.
5. Ella pagaría por viajar a la luna.

B. **Circle the correct form of the verb pagar. Then translate the sentences.**

1. No quiero que pagar/pagues por mi comida.
2. Siempre pago/paguéo mis tarjetas a tiempo.
3. Ayer le pagó/pagué diez dólares a mi vecino por lavarme el coche.
4. ¡Ya he paguido/pagado mi recibo de Internet!
5. Por favor, pague/paga la cuenta antes de irse.

C. **Complete the following sentences with the correct form of pagar.**

1. Te dije que no lo hicieras, pero no me hiciste caso... ¡y ahora _____ lo que rompiste!
   I told you not to do it, but you didn't listen to me... and now you will pay for what you broke!
2. Y pronto accedió a que se _____ un subsidio.
   And soon he agreed to pay a subsidy.
3. Siempre _____ por nuestros errores.
   We always pay for our mistakes.
4. _____ mi deuda a la universidad en diez años.
   I'll pay off my college debt in ten years.
5. ¿Cuánto te _____ por hacer ese trabajo?
   How much do you get paid to do that job?

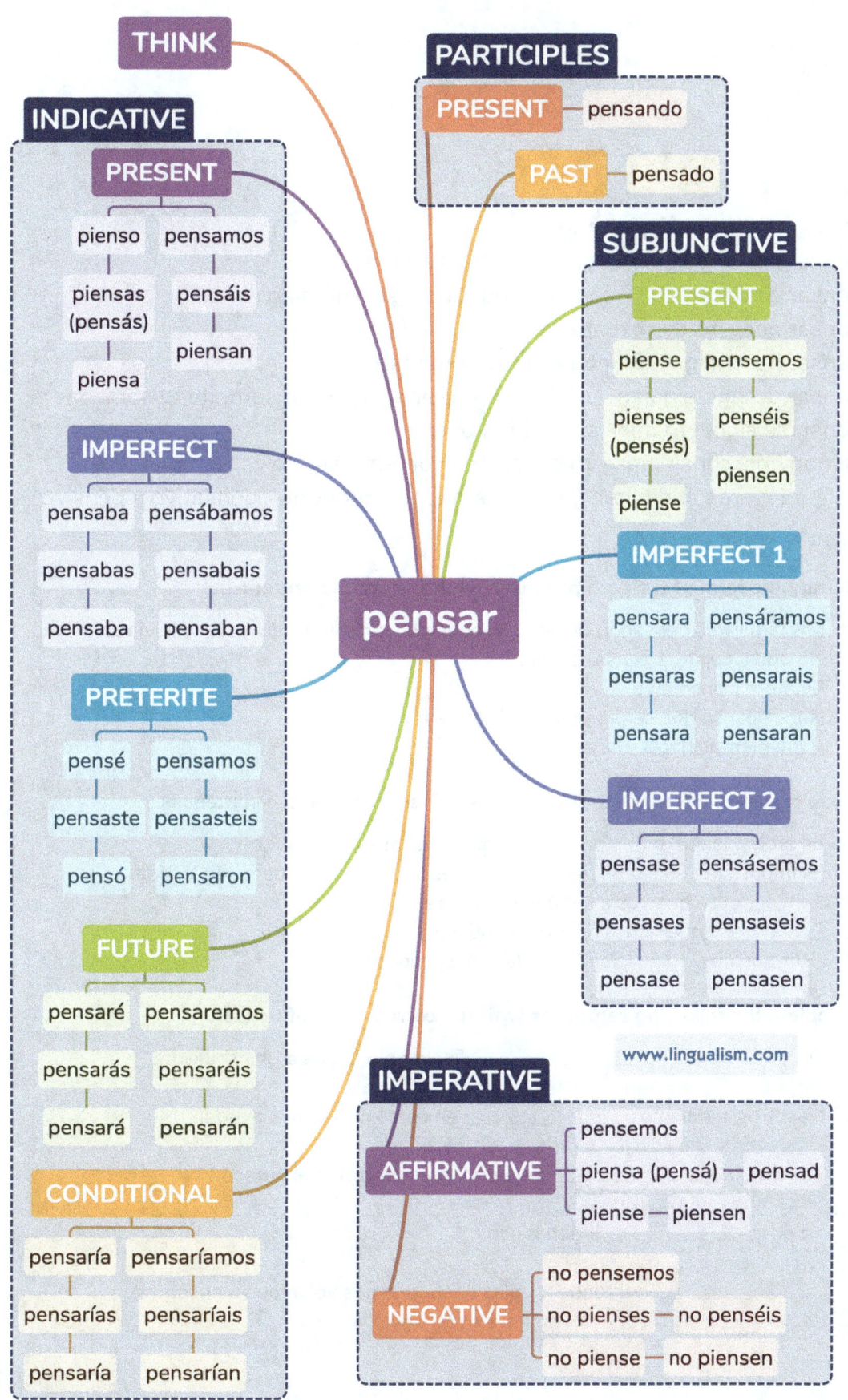

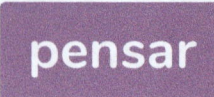

to think

stem-changing -ar verb: e → ie

- pensar en algo/alguien – to think about something
- pensar en hacer algo – to think about doing something
- pensar que – to think that...
- pensar hacer algo – to intend to do something
- pensar de algo/alguien – to think (have an opinion) of something/someone
- pensarse algo – to think something over
- (synonyms) considerar – to consider • contemplar – to contemplate
- (related words and idioms) el pensamiento – thought • pensativo – pensive

A. **Identify the form of the verb pensar. Then translate the sentences.**

1. Mis familiares pensaban que era un buen día para un paseo, pero la lluvia lo arruinó.
2. No podía dejar de pensar en ella.
3. Siempre pienso en ti.
4. Nunca pensé que sería tan difícil dejar de fumar.
5. ¿Qué piensas hacer mañana?

B. **Circle the correct form of the verb pensar. Then translate the sentences.**

1. Es probable que solo piénsara/pensara en sí mismo.
2. Es importante que penses/pienses qué es lo que quieres hacer en la vida.
3. Penso/Pienso que vas a ser un gran padre.
4. Pensé/Pince que nunca te vería de nuevo.
5. ¿Por qué no piences/piensas en las consecuencias?

C. **Complete the following sentences with the correct form of pensar.**

1. Después de mucho _____, finalmente llegué a una solución.
   After a lot of thinking, I finally came to a solution.
2. Nosotros estábamos _____ en cómo podríamos ayudar.
   We were thinking of how we could help.
3. Tristemente _____ que podríamos cambiar el mundo.
   Sadly, we thought we could change the world.
4. Yo no _____ ir a tu barco.
   I'm not going to go to your boat.
5. _____ en ti todos los días hasta que nos volvamos a encontrar.
   I will think of you every day until we meet again.

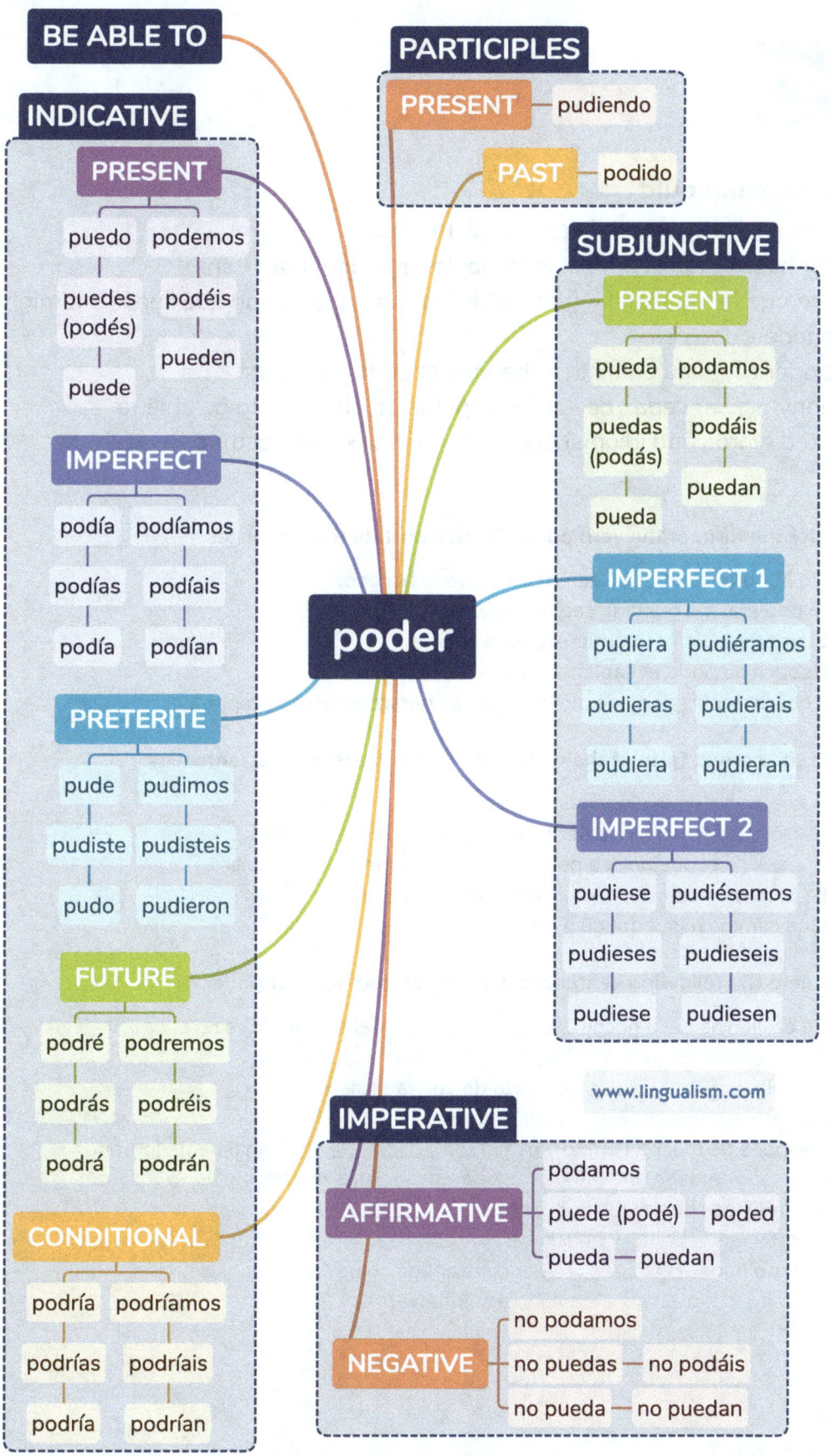

to be able to, can/could

irregular stem-changing -er verb: o → ue; pud-
- poder hacer – (ability) be able to do; (permission) may, can
- puede que (+ infinitive) – (possibility) may, might: Puede que llueva – It might rain.
- se puede – one can
- no poder con alguien – not to be able to stand someone
- (synonyms) ser capaz de – to be capable of • lograr – to be able to
- (related words and idioms) el poder – power • poderoso - powerful

A. **Identify the form of the verb poder. Then translate the sentences.**
1. No importa cuan difícil sea, sé que puedo hacerlo.
2. Si pudiera, me gustaría ser invisible.
3. Siempre podíamos contar el uno al otro.
4. Rebeca no pudo evitar llorar cuando lo vio.
5. Roberto tenía miedo de que sus padres nunca pudieran aceptarlo.

B. **Circle the correct form of the verb poder. Then translate the sentences.**
1. Pudía/Podía oír la alegría en su voz.
2. Podríamos/Pudemos haber sido amigos, pero ya es tarde.
3. Puede/Piede que no sea perfecta, pero es mi madre y la quiero.
4. La próxima vez podrás/pudiste hacerlo mejor.
5. Que camine hasta donde podrá/pueda.

C. **Complete the following sentences with the correct form of poder.**
1. En el silencio de la noche _____ oír el eco de mi voz.
   In the silence of the night I could hear the echo of my voice.
2. Tú sola _____ perderte de vuelta a casa.
   You alone could get lost on the way home.
3. Después de mucho tiempo y esfuerzo, _____ finalmente lograrlo.
   After a lot of time and effort, you were finally able to achieve it.
4. Andrés hace por nosotros cuanto _____.
   Andrés does for us as much as he can.
5. Aún no han _____ encontrar una solución.
   They have not been able to find a solution yet.

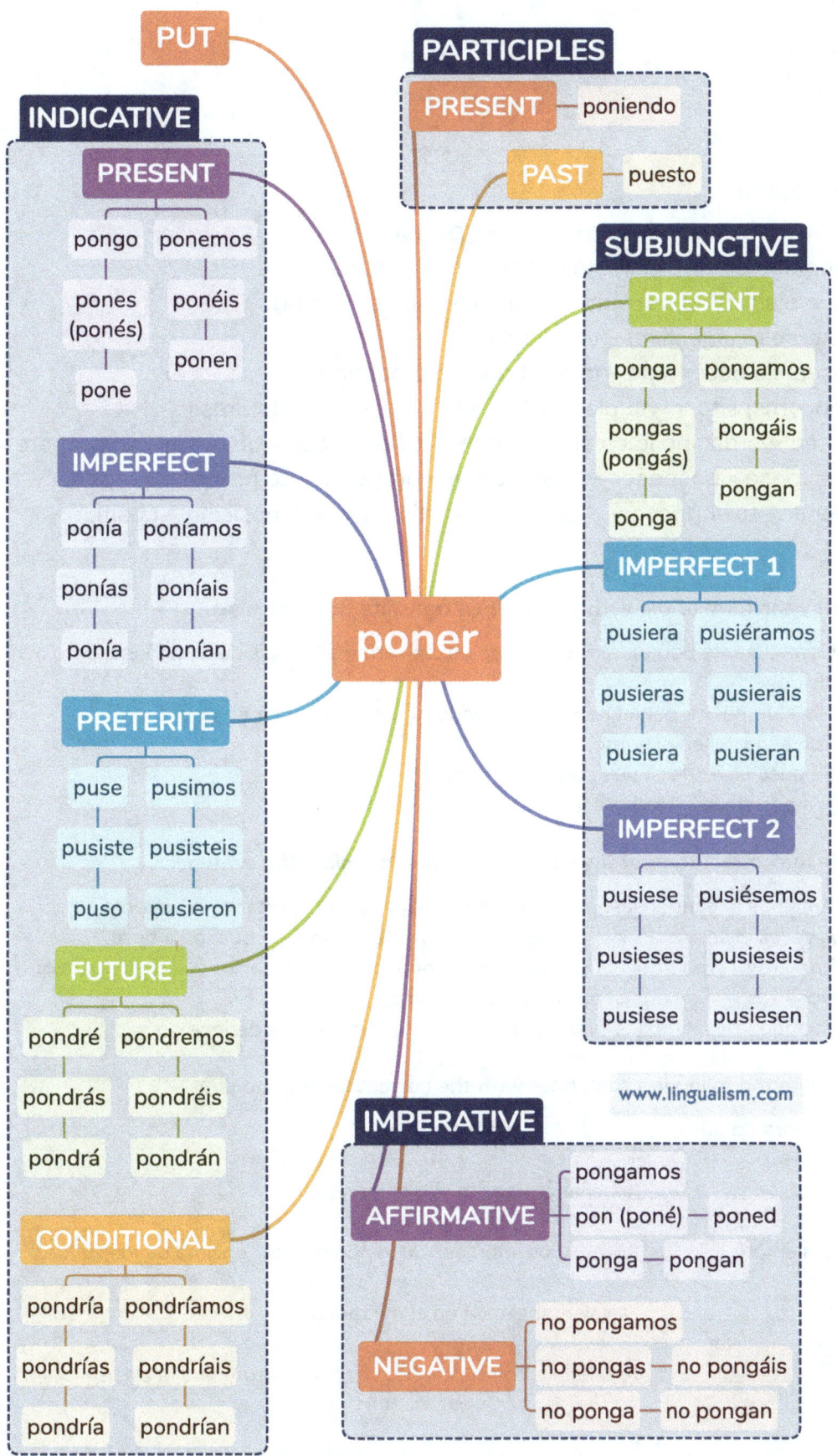

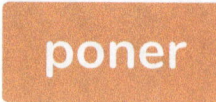

poner

to put, set, place

irregular -er verb: pong-, pus-, pond-, puest-
- poner algo en un lugar – to put something somewhere
- ponerse algo – to put something on, wear something
- ponserse (+ adjective) – to become
- ponserse a hacer algo – to start doing something
- (synonyms) situar – to place • fjiar – to set • vestir – to dress
- (related words and idioms) componer – to compose • disponer – to prepare • exponer – to expose • posponer – to postpone • proponer – to propose • reponer – to reply • suponer – to suppose • el puesto – position, job • la posición – position •

A. **Identify the form of the verb poner. Then translate the sentences.**
1. Normalmente pongo mi alarma para despertarme a las seis de la mañana, pero ayer se me olvidó.
2. Mis alumnos se ponen nerviosos cuando tienen que hablar en público.
3. Pon el pastel en el horno.
4. Se puso el vestido nuevo que le compré.
5. ¿Ya pusiste la mesa para la cena?

B. **Circle the correct form of the verb poner. Then translate the sentences.**
1. Antes de la pandemia, ponía/pusía mi alarma para despertarme a las siete.
2. A veces él se puso/ponía a meditar como recapacitando lo que iba a decir.
3. Primero pondrá/ponerá la comida en el horno y luego llamará a su familia para que cenen juntos.
4. Nosotras ponimos/pusimos los libros en la caja.
5. Cuando puenes/pones tu pecho junto al mío, el mundo se detiene.

C. **Complete the following sentences with the correct form of poner.**
1. Es hora de que _____ fin a eso.
   It's time we put an end to that.
2. Se _____ a bailar en cuanto oyó la música.
   He started dancing as soon as he heard the music.
3. Él siempre _____ los intereses de los demás por encima de los suyos.
   He always puts the interests of others above his own.
4. No _____ a calentar el café en el microondas.
   Don't heat up coffee in the microwave.
5. Si _____ tu teléfono en silencio, tal vez no interrumpiría la clase.
   If you put your phone on silent, maybe it wouldn't interrupt class.

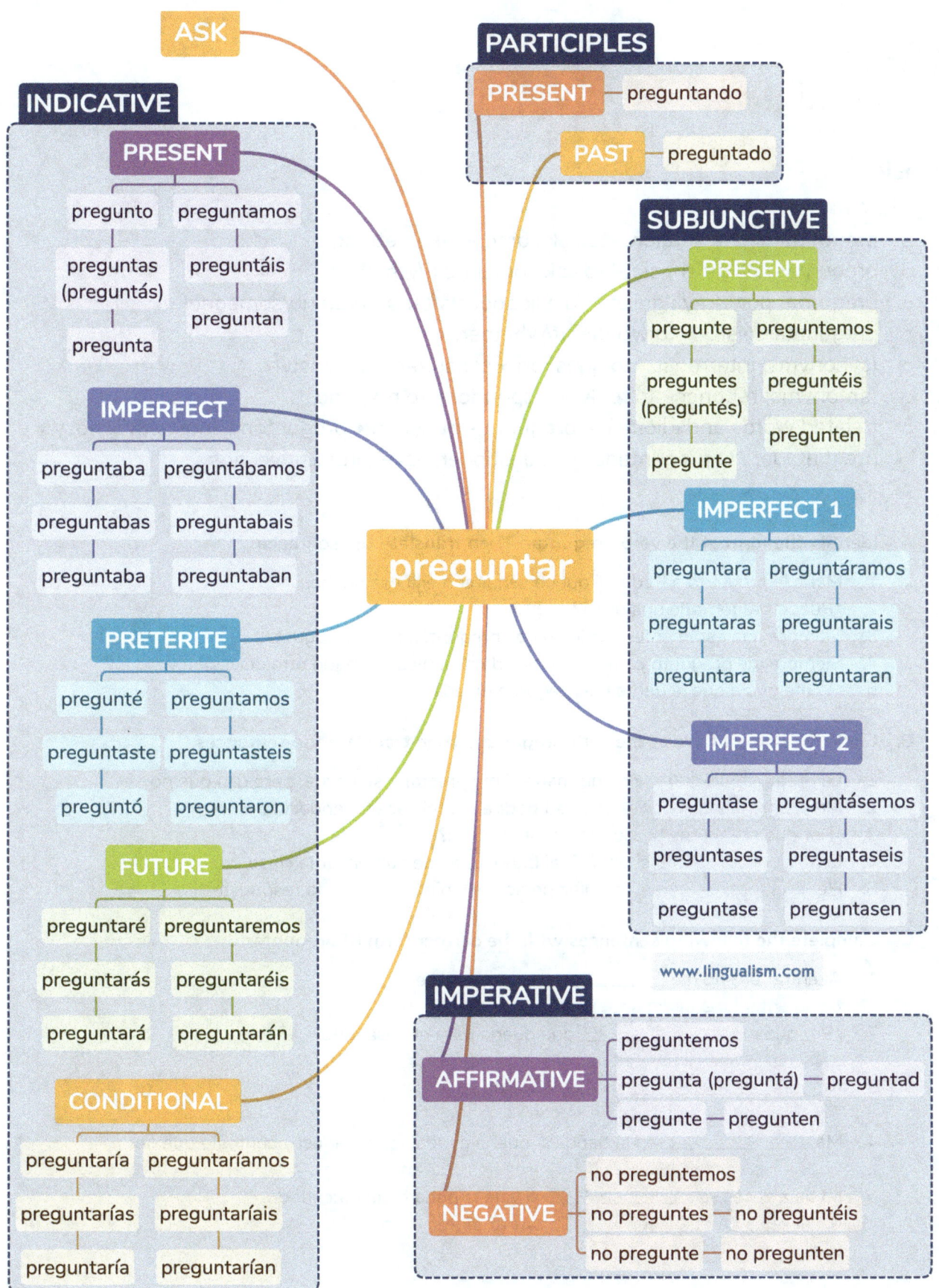

preguntar

to ask

regular -ar verb

- preguntar algo a alguien – to ask someone something
- preguntar (a alguien) si… – to ask someone if/whether…
- preguntar por algo/alguien – to ask about/after something/someone
- pregunatarse si… – to wonder if/whether…
- (synonyms) interrogar – to question • consultar – to consult
- (antonyms) reponer – to reply • responder – to respond
- (related words and idioms) la pregunta – question • preguntón – inquisitive, nosy • el preguntador / la preguntadora – questioner, asker; inquisitive, nosy

A. Identify the form of the verb preguntar. Then translate the sentences.

1. María le preguntó a Pedro si quería cenar con ella esa noche.
2. ¿Puedo preguntarle una duda?
3. Siempre que están enfermos los niños preguntan por sus juguetes.
4. Siempre me pregunto cómo sería mi vida si hubiese tomado otra decisión.
5. No me gusta que la gente me pregunte mi edad.

B. Circle the correct form of the verb preguntar. Then translate the sentences.

1. Le pregunté/pregunto a mi hermana si me prestaba su coche, pero dijo que no.
2. Me preguntaba/preguntía si usted podría ir a mi casa y bendecirla.
3. ¿Por qué preguntas/preguentas tantas cosas?
4. Él preguntá/preguntó si podía ir al baño antes de comenzar la clase.
5. He preguntado/preguntar a diez personas y ninguna sabía la respuesta.

C. Complete the following sentences with the correct form of preguntar.

1. Al entrar ella no me _____ mi nombre.
   Upon entering she did not ask my name.
2. ¿Por qué me _____ qué quería para el desayuno?
   Why did you ask me what I wanted for breakfast?
3. No me _____ si estoy enojado.
   Don't ask me if I'm angry.
4. Me _____ en la tienda si quería ayuda, les agradecí y contesté que no.
   They asked me at the store if I wanted help, I thanked them and said no.
5. Mi tía a veces se _____ si vale la pena seguir luchando.
   My aunt sometimes wonders if it's worth fighting on.

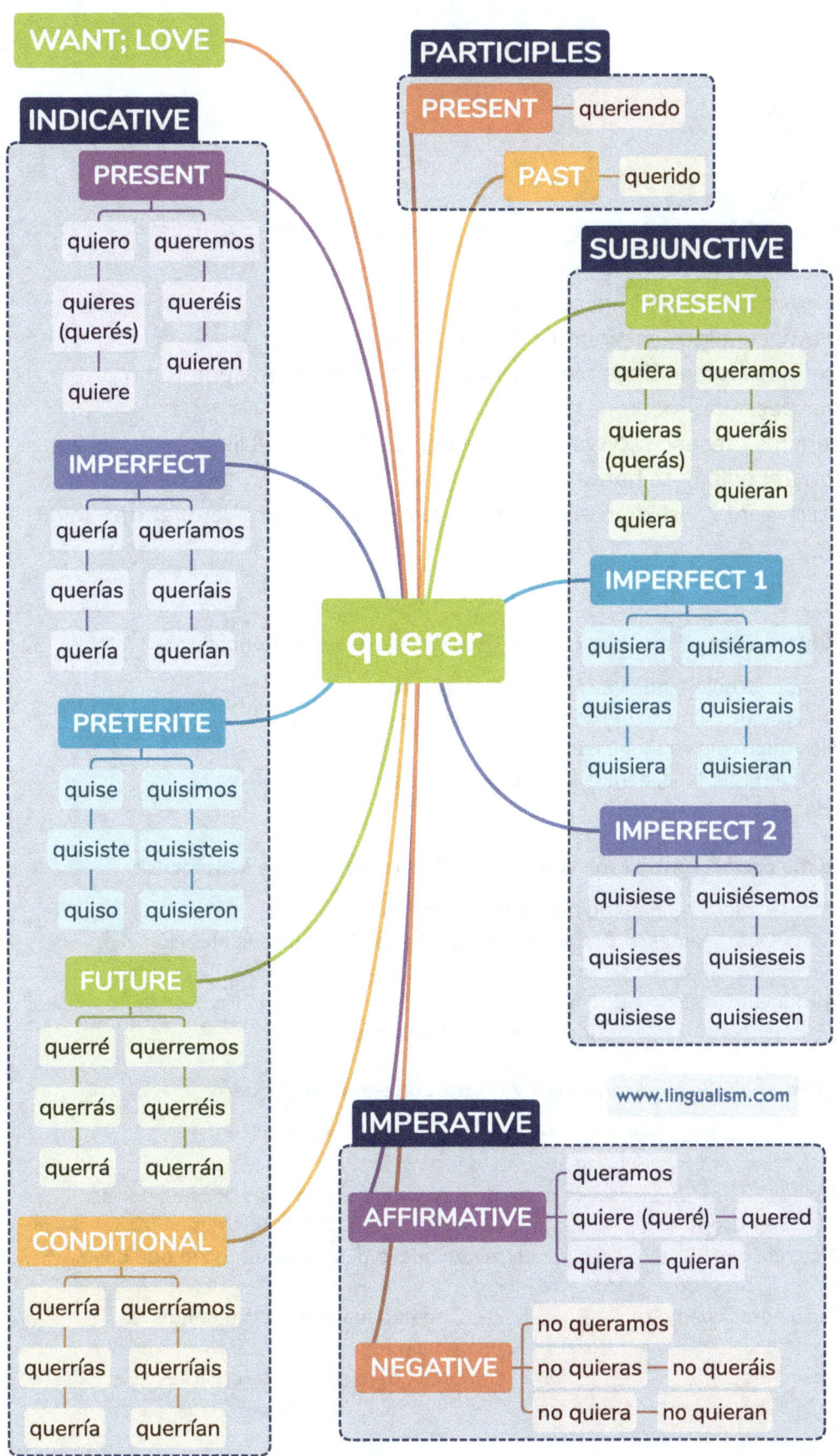

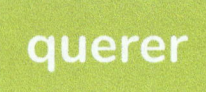

querer

to want; to love

irregular stem-changing -er verb: e → ie; quis-, querr-
- querer algo – to want something
- querer a alguien – to love someone
- querer hacer algo – to want to do something
- querer que alguien haga algo – to want someone to do something
- querer decir – to mean
- (synonyms) desear – to want • tener ganas de – to feel like
- (antonym) odiar – to hate
- (related words and idioms) el querer – love • el querido / la querida – lover, sweetheart; dear __

A. Identify the form of the verb querer. Then translate the sentences.
1. Mi abuela quiere que vaya a visitarla mañana.
2. Quiero que mi novio me compre un anillo de diamantes.
3. Nos querremos aunque estemos lejos.
4. Yo quería ser feliz, pero la felicidad es un estado de ánimo.
5. ¡Haz lo que quieras!

B. Circle the correct form of the verb querer. Then translate the sentences.
1. Te querro/quiero, pero no puedo estar contigo.
2. Querí/Quería ser escritora, pero la actuación me llamó más la atención.
3. Siempre quiso/quise ser una persona de éxito, y ahora lo soy.
4. Aunque no quiéramos/queramos, tenemos que terminar el informe hoy.
5. ¿Quieres/Quisieres ir al cine conmigo esta noche?

C. Complete the following sentences with the correct form of querer.
1. ¿_____ ser mi amigo cuando estemos viejos?
   Will you want to be my friend when we're old?
2. No _____ escuchar, así que ahora vas a pagar las consecuencias.
   You didn't want to listen, so now you're going to pay the consequences.
3. No creía que _____ verme de nuevo después de todo lo que pasó.
   I didn't think you wanted to see me again after everything that happened.
4. Si supieras cuanto te _____, no dudarías para estar conmigo.
   If you knew how much I love you, you would not hesitate to be with me.
5. Los niños _____ ver el atardecer, pero se durmieron antes.
   The children wanted to see the sunset, but they fell asleep before.

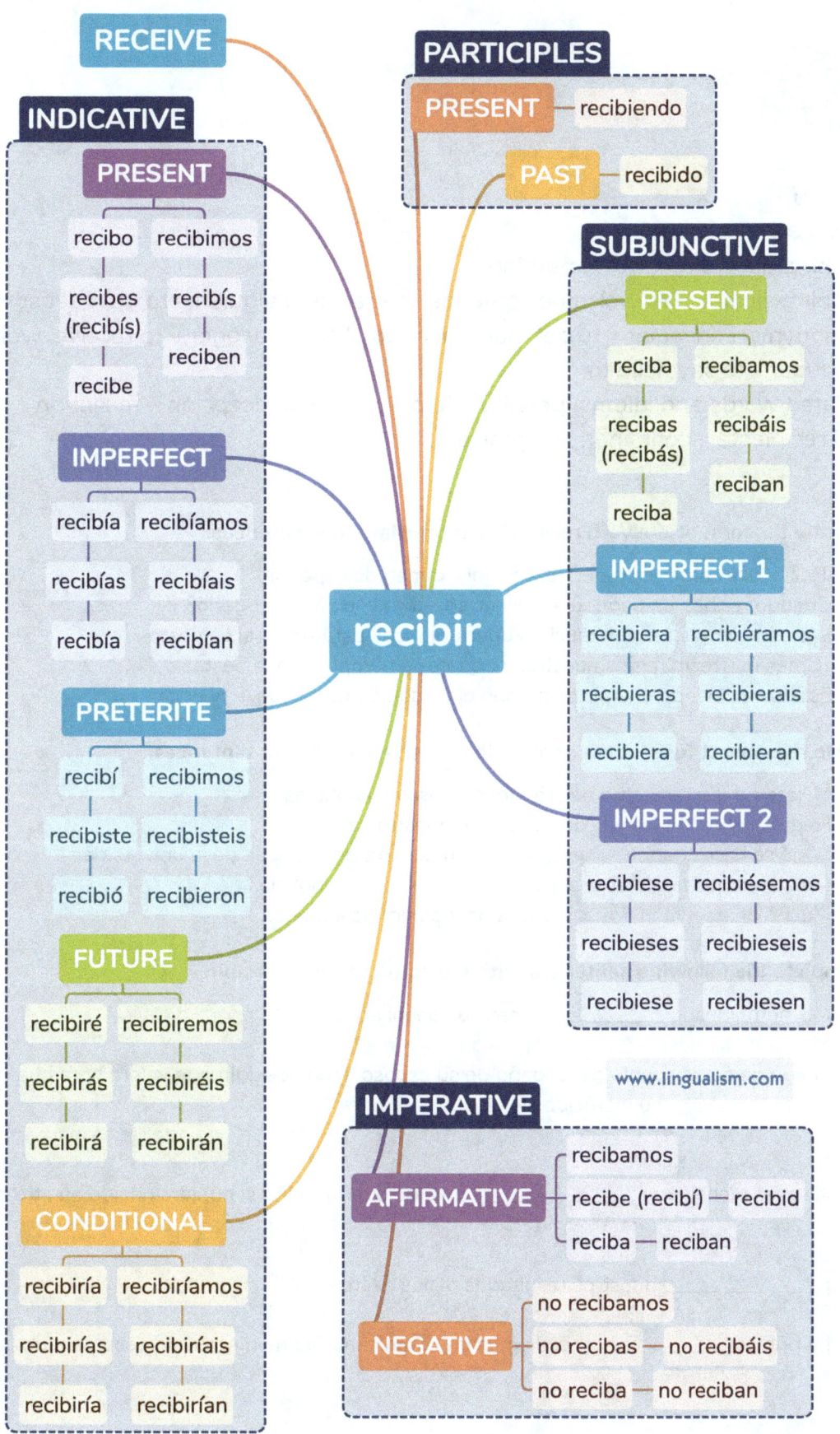

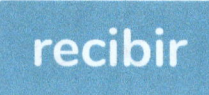

to receive, get
regular -ir verb

- recibir algo – to receive something
- recibir a alguien – to welcome someone; ir a recibir a alguien – to go meet someone
- (synonyms) conseguir – to get • obtener – to obtain • acoger – to receive, welcome • saludar – to say hello to
- (related words and idioms) percibir – to perceive • la recepción – reception • el recipiente – container, receptacle

A. **Identify the form of the verb recibir. Then translate the sentences.**
   1. ¡Recibí una calificación perfecta en mi examen de español!
   2. Cuando recibes un paquete en el correo, ¿tardas en ir a recogerlo?
   3. Los estudiantes reciben muchas oportunidades para pasar el semestre.
   4. ¿Crees que recibiremos nuestros paquetes a tiempo para la fiesta?
   5. Estaba recibiendo una pizza cuando oí un sonido detrás de la puerta.

B. **Circle the correct form of the verb recibir. Then translate the sentences.**
   1. Mi jefe recibió/recibo un paquete misterioso en la oficina.
   2. Hemos recibidos/recibido un regalo de nuestros abuelos.
   3. ¿Qué se hace cuando reciebes/recibes una carta de /rechazo de la universidad?
   4. Me alegra que finalmente recibiéramos/recibimos la noticia.
   5. Mucha gente reciben/recibe ayuda del gobierno cada año.

C. **Complete the following sentences with the correct form of recibir.**
   1. Mis hermanos _____ regalos de mi abuela.
      My brothers received gifts from my grandmother.
   2. Luego de darse cuenta del engaño de su esposo, María decidió que ya era hora que él _____ su merecido.
      After noticing her husband's deception, María decided that it was time for him to get what he deserved from her.
   3. A veces pienso que _____ una mejor educación si hubiera nacido en otro país.
      Sometimes I think that I would have received a better education if I had been born in another country.
   4. ¡_____ nuestros resultados de los exámenes!
      We received our test results!
   5. Mi prima _____ cada mes una gran cantidad de dinero, sin saber su origen.
      My cousin received a large amount of money every month, without knowing its origin.

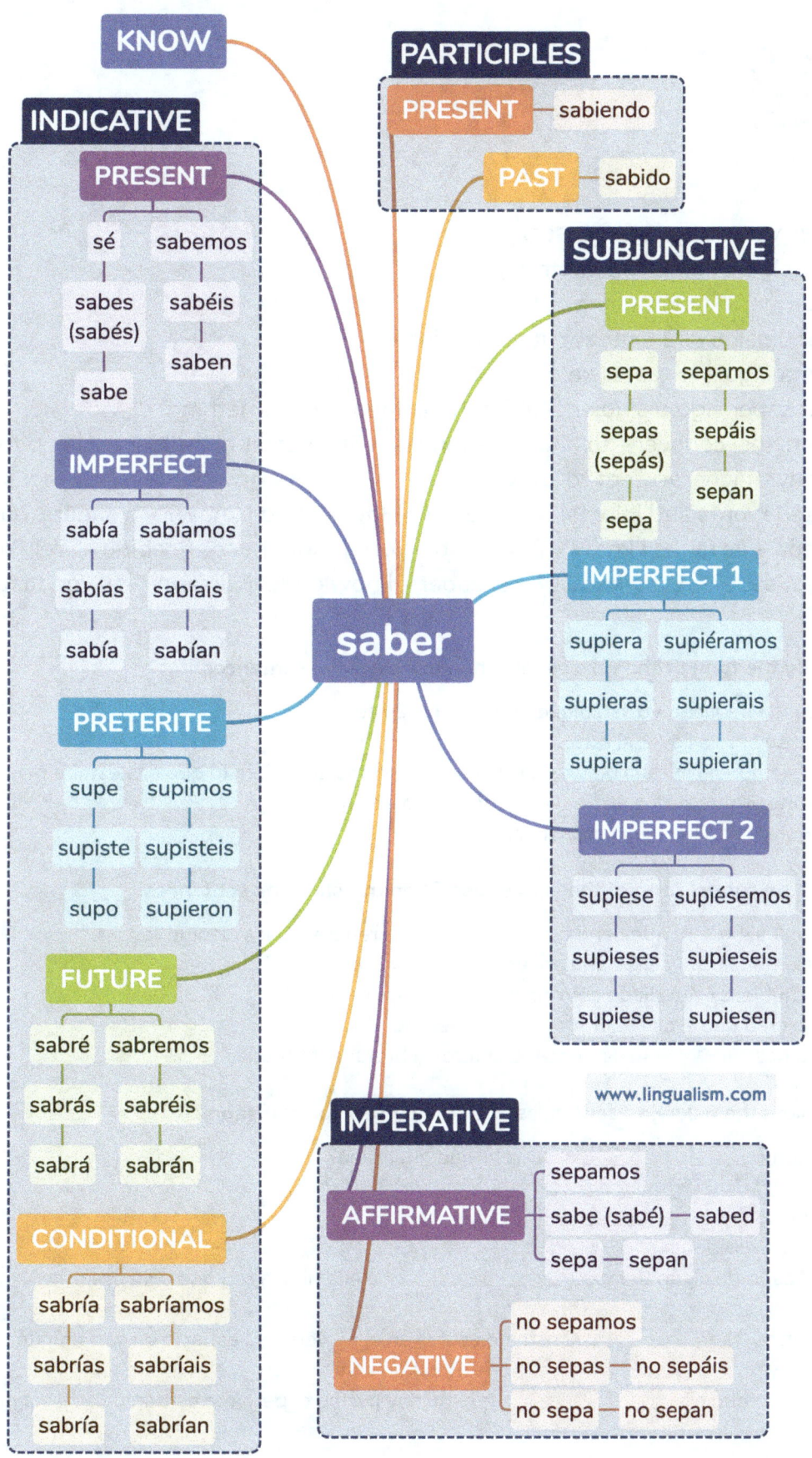

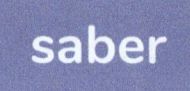

saber

to know

irregular -er verb: sup, sabr-, sep-
- saber algo – to know something
- saber que... - to know that...
- saber de algo – to hear about something
- saber a algo – to taste like
- hacer saber algo a alguien – to inform someone of something
- (synonyms) conocer – to know, be familiar with • estar al tanto – to be up to date
- (antonym) ignorar – not to know
- (related words and idioms) ¡Qué sé yo! – How should I know? • a saber – namely • que yo sepa – as far as I know • ¡Ya lo sabía yo! – I thought so! • sabido – well-known • ¿Quién sabe? – Who knows? • el saber – knowledge • el sabor – flavor, taste

A. Identify the form of the verb saber. Then translate the sentences.

1. Desde pequeño yo sabía que quería ser médico.
2. No sé si va a llover al rato.
3. Él siempre la miraba de una forma especial, como si supiera lo que ella estaba pensando.
4. Nunca sabré si lo que me dijo fue verdad o una mentira.
5. ¿Por qué no me lo hiciste saber?

B. Circle the correct form of the verb saber. Then translate the sentences.

1. (Ella) sabe/sabi que tiene que estudiar pero prefiere jugar videojuegos.
2. ¿Cómo supiste/sepas que era yo?
3. Si hubieses estudiado astronomía sabrías/sabrás eso.
4. No creo que ellos sabían/supieran la verdad.
5. Tú has sabido/supusto vencer esa feroz y brutal enfermedad.

C. Complete the following sentences with the correct form of saber.

1. ¿Cómo _____ el secreto que guardaba?
   How did you know the secret I was keeping?
2. El vino tinto _____ a frutas.
   Red wine tastes of fruits.
3. Al cabo de algún tiempo _____ que ella nunca regresó a su casa.
   After some time, we learned that she never returned to her house.
4. Nunca _____ si estamos solos en el universo. El espacio es casi infinito.
   We will never know if we are alone in the universe. Outer space is almost infinite.
5. Quiero que ella _____ que no soy perfecto, pero me esfuerzo cada día por ser mejor.
   I want her to know that I am not perfect, but I strive every day to be better.

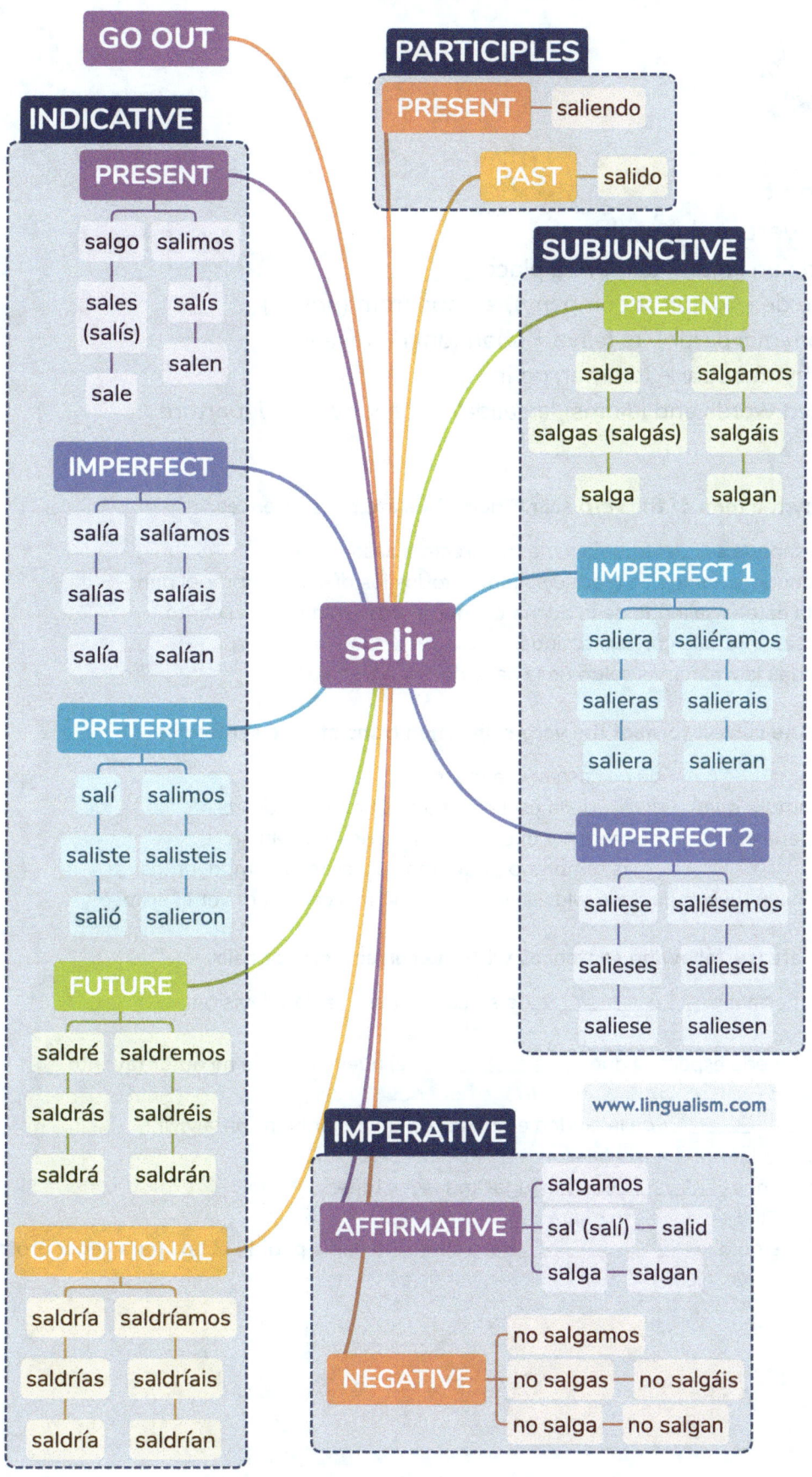

salir

to go out, exit

irregular -ir verb: salg-, sald-
- salir de un lugar – to leave a place
- salirse de – to quit (a company), escape from (prison)
- (synonyms) partir – to leave • abandonar – to leave
- (antonym) entrar – to enter, go in
- (related words and idioms) la salida – exit, way out; departure

A. Identify the form of the verb salir. Then translate the sentences.

1. El sábado salí del trabajo y me fui directo a casa.
2. Cuando vivíamos en Madrid salíamos todos los días a comprar el pan.
3. Ella estaba saliendo de la ducha cuando oyó un ruido y se espantó.
4. Él siempre sale con sus amigos.
5. Todas las mañanas salgo de la casa para ir a trabajar.

B. Circle the correct form of the verb salir. Then translate the sentences.

1. ¡Salgan/Salguen de mi casa ahora mismo!
2. Siempre que salía/salió de la escuela, iba a la tienda de dulces.
3. Apenas salí/salé de casa, me di cuenta que olvidé mi celular.
4. Si salgas/salieras más temprano podríamos pasar más tiempo juntos.
5. Si no estuviera nublado ellos salirían/saldrían a la calle para ver el eclipse.

C. Complete the following sentences with the correct form of salir.

1. Mi hermano _____ de su cuarto para ver la televisión.
   My brother left his room to watch television.
2. No puedo esperar a que _____ el nuevo libro de mi autor favorito.
   I can't wait for my favorite author's new book to come out.
3. _____ de la ciudad en busca de un mejor lugar para vivir.
   We will leave the city in search of a better place to live.
4. Los niños _____ a jugar todas las tardes.
   The children go out to play every afternoon.
5. Antes de que _____ del trabajo, ya había pedido el taxi para llegar pronto a casa.
   Before we left work, he had already ordered the taxi to get home quickly.

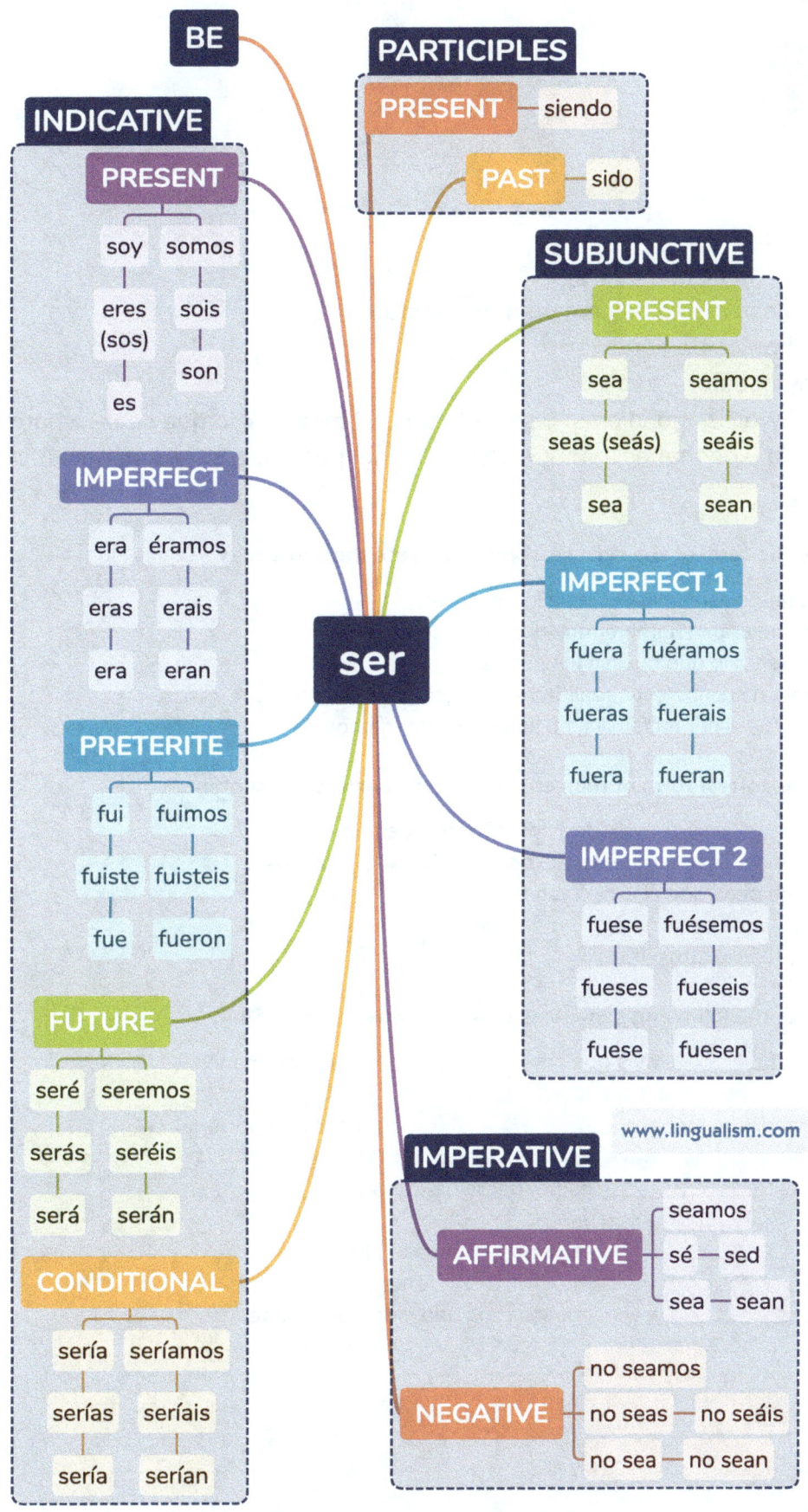

to be

irregular -er verb

- ser algo – to be something
- ser + adjective – to be (in a permanent state)
- ser hecho – to be done
- (synonym) estar – to be
- (related words and idioms) o sea – that is…, I mean… • lo que sea – whatever • sea como sea – be that as it may • el ser – being, person: el ser humano – human being

A. Identify the form of the verb ser. Then translate the sentences.

1. Los gatos son animales muy inteligentes.
2. Enrique era un hombre muy rico, pero no era feliz.
3. ¿Qué será lo que buscan los perros?
4. Sería un sueño hecho realidad si pudiera ganar la lotería.
5. Si no fuera por mi familia, no sé dónde estaría hoy.

B. Circle the correct form of the verb ser. Then translate the sentences.

1. No séremos/seremos estudiantes todo el tiempo.
2. Es imposible ignorar el hecho de que ella es/sea hermosa.
3. Es una pena que él es/sea tan tonto.
4. Sé/Soy una persona muy ordenada.
5. ¡No seas/ses grosero!

C. Complete the following sentences with the correct form of ser.

1. _____ más que amigos; _____ hermanos.
   We are more than friends; we are brothers.
2. Mi madre siempre ha _____ un gran apoyo emocional.
   My mother has always been a great emotional support.
3. Antes _____ compañeros de trabajo.
   We used to be co-workers.
4. _____ mi primer amor y nunca te olvidaré.
   You were my first love, and I will never forget you.
5. _____ joven y tienes toda una vida por delante.
   You are young, and you have a whole life ahead of you.

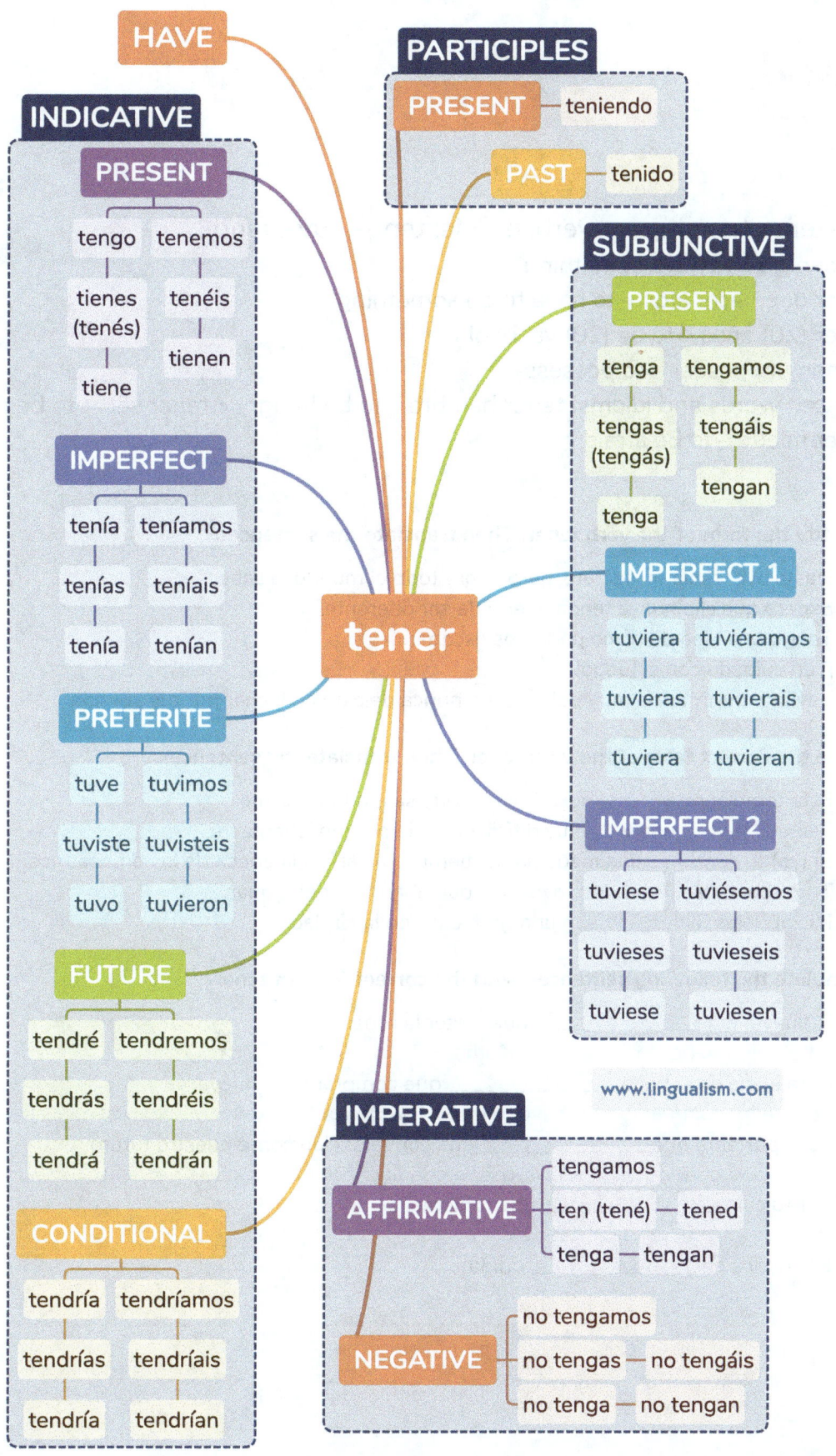

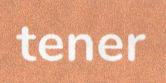

tener

to have

irregular stem-changing -er verb: e → ie; teng-, tuv-, tend-
- tener algo – to have something
- tener que hacer algo – to have to do something
- tener (20) años – to be (20) years old
- (synonym) poseer – to possess
- (related words and idioms) tener hambre – to be hungry • tener sed – to be thirsty • tener miedo – to be afraid

A. **Identify the form of the verb tener. Then translate the sentences.**
1. Hasta ayer tenía un secreto, pero ahora todo el mundo lo sabe.
2. Espero que ella nunca tenga miedo de ser diferente.
3. Tengo una idea de cómo podemos escapar.
4. ¡Ten cuidado con el fuego!
5. Tuviste una infancia muy pobre, pero nunca dejaste de luchar por tus sueños.

B. **Circle the correct form of the verb tener. Then translate the sentences.**
1. Está temblando y tengamos/tenemos que salir ahora mismo.
2. Teniste/Tuviste una vida muy difícil, pero siempre te levantaste.
3. Si (yo) tuviera/tuve una máquina del tiempo, viajaría a la época de los dinosaurios.
4. Tras el huracán, Armando tovo/tuvo que abandonar su hogar.
5. Mis abuelos tuvieron/tenían una gran casa en la ciudad.

C. **Complete the following sentences with the correct form of tener.**
1. Si llueve, (tú) _____ que meter la ropa.
   If it rains, you have to pack your clothes.
2. Para el día de la boda _____ que comprar ropa nueva.
   For the wedding day, I will have to buy new clothes.
3. Es importante que _____ una conversación sobre nuestro futuro.
   It is important that we have a conversation about our future.
4. Por tu culpa _____ un problema.
   Because of you, we have a problem.
5. Ella nunca ha _____ un gato.
   She has never had a cat.

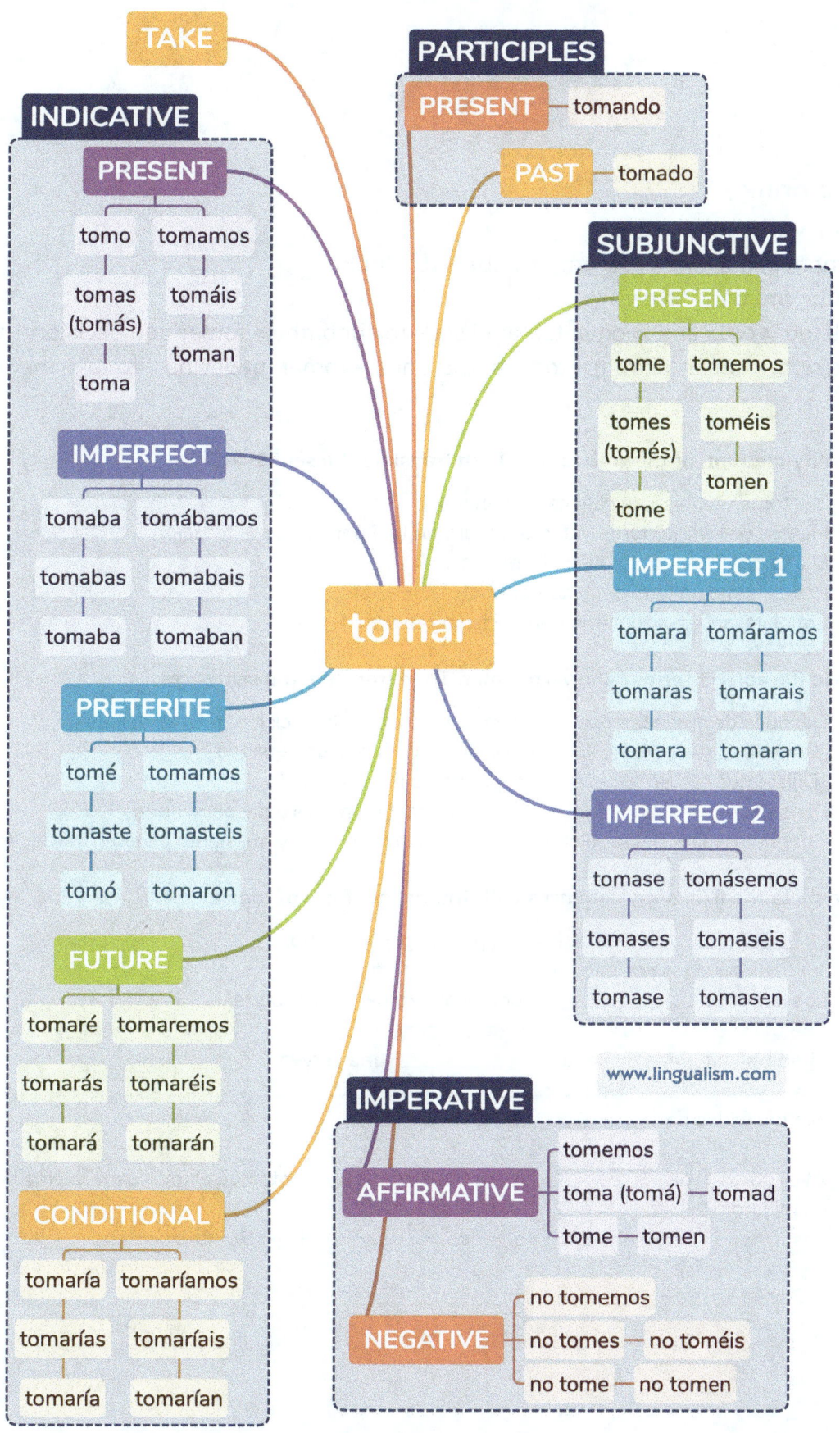

to take; to drink
regular -ar verb
- (synonyms) agarrar – to grab • beber – to drink
- (antonym) dar – to give
- (related words and idioms) tomar el sol – to sunbathe • tomar una decisión – to make a decision • tomar (el tren) – to take (the train) • tomar medecina – to take medicine

A. Identify the form of the verb tomar. Then translate the sentences.
1. Ella toma una taza de café cada mañana.
2. Marcos se levantó tarde y ahora tomará un taxi para llegar al trabajo.
3. Ella tomó su mano y le dijo: "Te quiero".
4. Pase y tome un libro del estante.
5. Era necesario que tomaran una decisión rápida.

B. Circle the correct form of the verb tomar. Then translate the sentences.
1. Después de mucho pensar, finalmente tumé/tomé la decisión de irme del país.
2. ¿Por qué tomaste/tomastes la decisión de no ir a la universidad?
3. ¿Dijiste que tomás/tomabas medicamentos para dormir?
4. Pensaba que los niños tomarían/tomarán mi dinero, pero me equivoqué.
5. Cuando termino de trabajar tomé/tomo mi taza de café y me siento a ver el atardecer.

C. Complete the following sentences with the correct form of tomar.
1. _____ el tren de las seis para llegar a tiempo.
   We'll take the six o'clock train to get there on time.
2. Los ladrones _____ todo el dinero de la caja fuerte.
   The thieves took all the money from the safe.
3. Si no trabajáramos mañana _____ una cerveza.
   If we weren't working tomorrow, we'd have a beer.
4. ¡No te olvides de _____ tu medicina!
   Don't forget to take your medicine!
5. Ayer que estaba _____ un café en el patio, noté que el gato de la vecina había estado en mi jardín.
   Yesterday when I was having coffee on the patio, I noticed that the neighbor's cat had been in my garden.

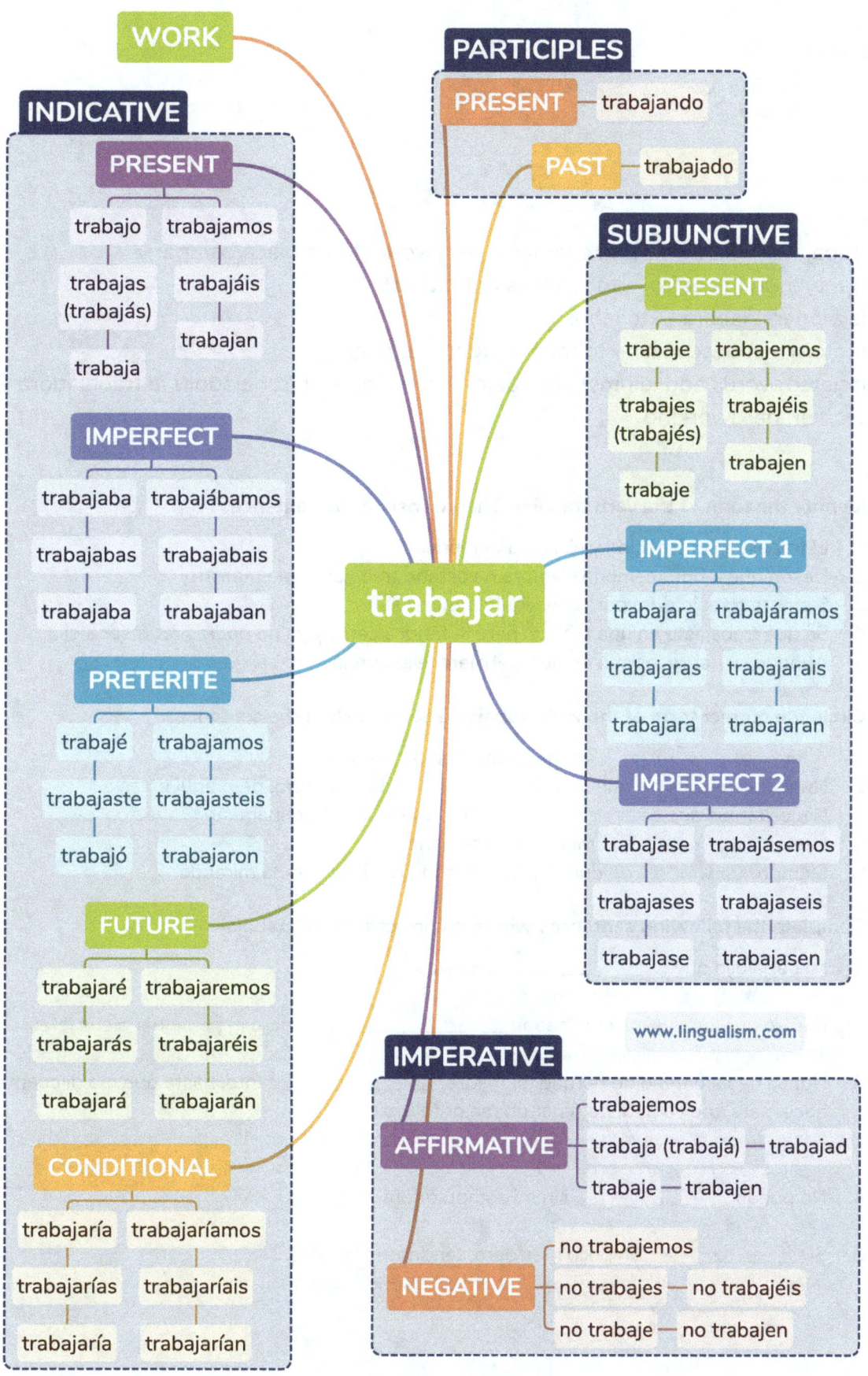

91 • Need-to-Know Spanish Verbs – Book 1

trabajar

to work
regular -ar verb

- trabajar en un lugar / una compañía – to work at/in a place/company
- trabajar de (maestro) – to work as a (teacher)
- (synonym) laborar – to labor
- (antonyms) descansar – to relax • jugar – to play
- (related words and idioms) el trabajo – work, job • el trabajador / la trabajadora – worker; hardworking

A. **Identify the form of the verb trabajar. Then translate the sentences.**
1. Él trabaja en una oficina y ella en una fábrica.
2. Desde que tengo memoria siempre he estado trabajando de maestro.
3. Siempre trabajo duro para conseguir lo que quiero.
4. Sé que trabajaste en una fábrica, pero la fábrica cerró y ya no podrás regresar a ella.
5. Aunque su padre insistió en que trabajara, ella quería estudiar.

B. **Circle the correct form of the verb trabajar. Then translate the sentences.**
1. Ayer trabajamos/trabajemos hasta las diez de la noche.
2. Nunca te imaginaste que trabajaría/trabajarías de camarera, pero aquí estás.
3. Necesitamos que trabajamos/trabajemos juntos para terminar este proyecto.
4. He trabajado/trabajando mucho esta semana.
5. Siempre trabajó/trajabó duro, incluso cuando nadie la estaba mirando.

C. **Complete the following sentences with the correct form of trabajar.**
1. Mi papá dijo que _____ demasiado.
   My dad said we worked too hard.
2. Pienso que los nuevos empleados _____ duro para impresionar a sus jefes.
   I think new hires will work hard to impress their bosses.
3. Nunca había entendido porqué mi madre _____ tanto, hasta que me di cuenta que lo hacía para que yo pudiera tener un mejor futuro.
   I had never understood why my mother worked so hard, until I realized that she did it so that I could have a better future.
4. No puedo _____ sin mi computadora.
   I can't work without my computer.
5. Si _____ un poco más duro, tendrías más éxito.
   If you worked a little harder, you would be more successful.

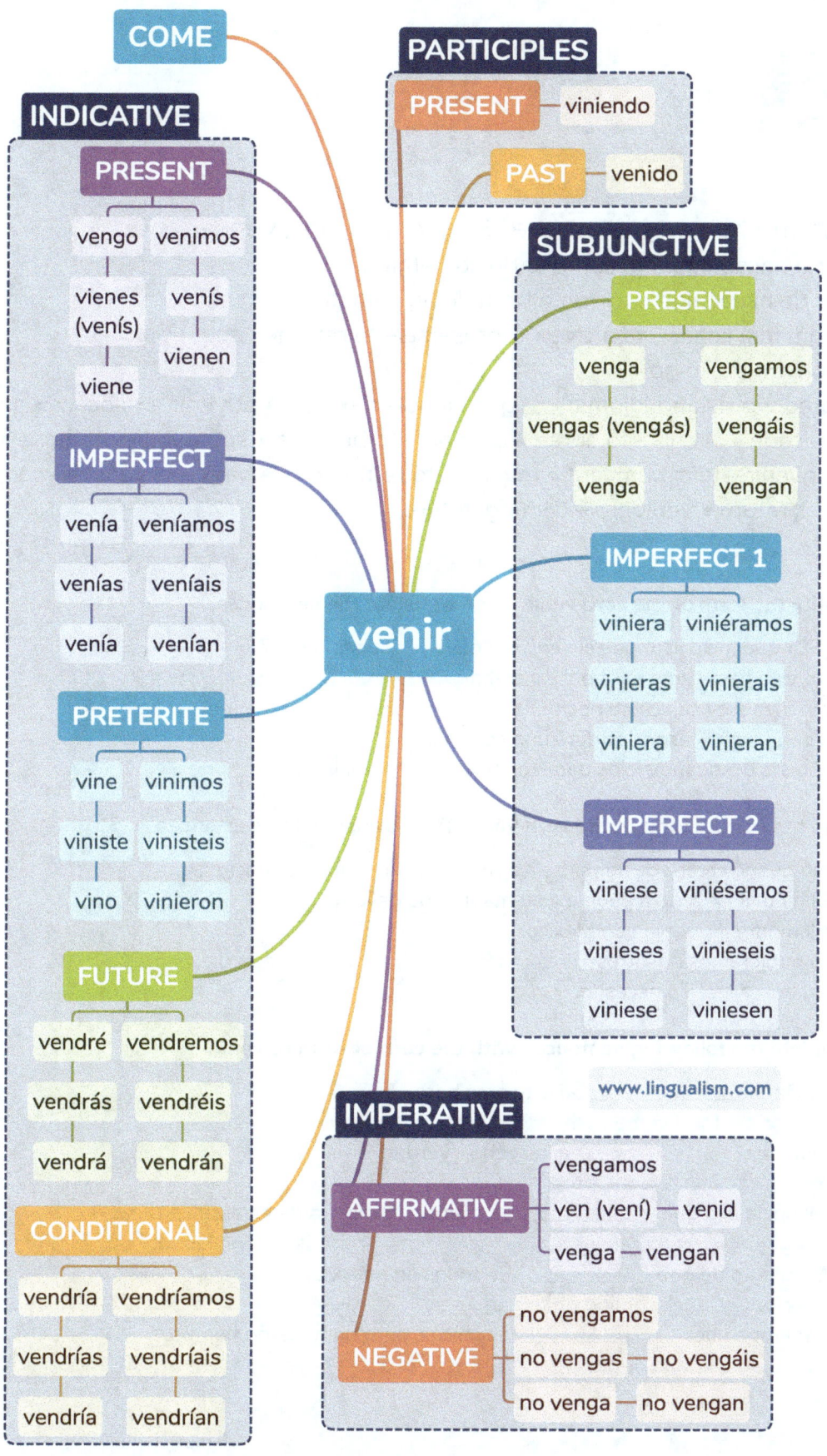

to come

irregular stem-changing -ir verb: e → ie; veng-, vin-, vend-
- venir a hacer algo – to come to do something
- venir de hacer algo – to come from doing something
- (synonyms) llegar – to arrive • regresarse – to return
- (antonym) ir – to go
- (related words and idioms) ___ que viene – next ___ • advenir – to occur • antevenir – to precede • avenir – to agree • devenir – to become • sobrevenir – to arise • circunvenir – to circumvent • revenir – to return, come back • la venida – coming, arrival, return • venidero – coming, future

A. Identify the form of the verb venir. Then translate the sentences.
1. ¿Por qué me dijiste que sí venías si no lo pensabas hacer?
2. Yo vine hasta aquí para buscar trabajo.
3. ¿Vienes a mi casa esta noche?
4. Vengan a mi casa y les daré una sorpresa.
5. Viniste desde muy lejos para ver este hermoso paisaje.

B. Circle the correct form of the verb venir. Then translate the sentences.
1. No puedo creer que mi padre no venga/vendrá a mi graduación.
2. El niño venió/vino a pedirle a su madre una galleta.
3. Mi madre viene/vine de México.
4. Si pudiéramos nosotros vengamos/vendríamos a verte cada día.
5. ¡Vengas/Ven! Te necesito.

C. Complete the following sentences with the correct form of venir.
1. Mañana _____ a la misma hora.
   Tomorrow I will come at the same time.
2. Ustedes _____ a las ocho, ¿verdad?
   You're coming at eight, right?
3. Mi novia dijo que _____ cuando terminara de lavar.
   My girlfriend said that she would come when she finished the laundry.
4. Me alegro de que _____ todos en este viaje.
   I'm glad we're all coming on this trip.
5. Esperaba que _____ las chicas, pero no tuvieron tiempo.
   I was waiting for the girls to come, but they didn't have time.

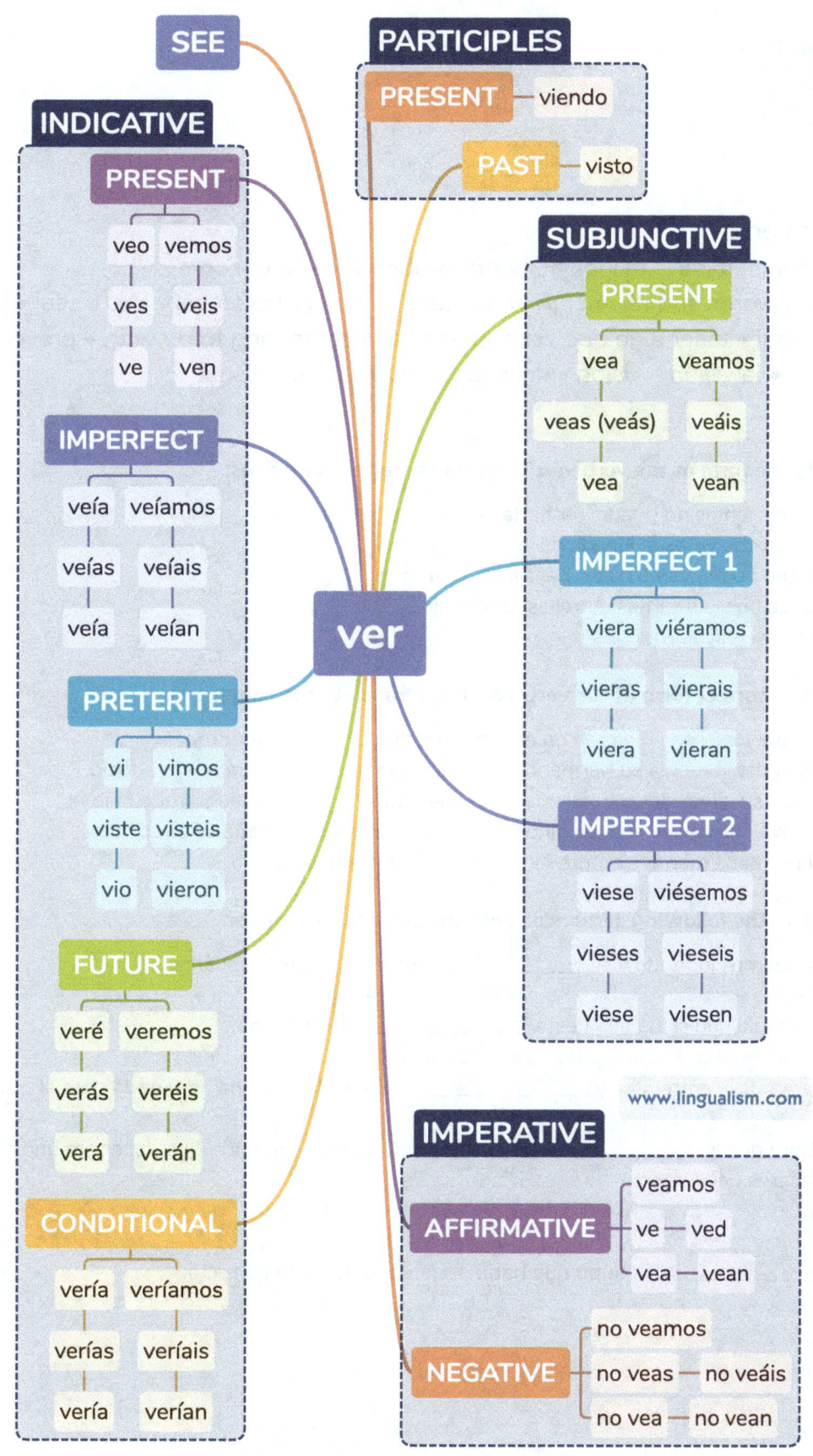

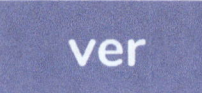

to see

irregular -er verb: vi-
- (synonyms) mirar – to look at, watch • observar – to observe
- (related words and idioms) ¡A ver! – Let's see! • ¡Ya veremos! – We'll see! • ¡Nos vemos! – See you! • tener algo que ver con – to have something to do with • prever – to foresee • la visión – vision • la vista – view • visual – visual

A. Identify the form of the verb ver. Then translate the sentences.
1. Sin mis lentes no puedo ver nada.
2. Esta noche verás la luna llena.
3. Se que no me vas a creer, pero ayer vi un ovni.
4. Nunca he visto tantas estrellas en el cielo.
5. ¿Ves ese coche rojo? ¡Es mío!

B. Circle the correct form of the verb ver. Then translate the sentences.
1. María y José se ven/vieron en el supermercado y no se saludaron.
2. Alejandra vio/vió a su hermano en la calle con una mujer que no reconoció.
3. Miró a su alrededor para asegurarse que nadie la ve/viera, luego robó la joya.
4. A través de la ventana los niños veían/veyan la tormenta que se avecinaba.
5. Mi hermana menor siempre vie/ve las películas antes que yo.

C. Complete the following sentences with the correct form of ver.
1. Estabamos jugando y _____ a un gato negro en el árbol.
   We were playing, and we saw a black cat in the tree.
2. Ella sabía que si iba a la fiesta, _____ a mi amigo.
   She knew that if she went to the party, she would see my friend.
3. Haremos la entrevista y _____ si ella es la persona adecuada para el trabajo.
   We'll do the interview and see if she's the right person for the job.
4. Ahora que lo _____ en retrospectiva, no tener nada que hacer era uno de los mayores placeres del verano.
   Now that I look back, not having anything to do was one of the greatest pleasures of the summer.
5. Al _____, supo que había tomado la decisión correcta.
   Seeing him, she knew that she had made the right decision.

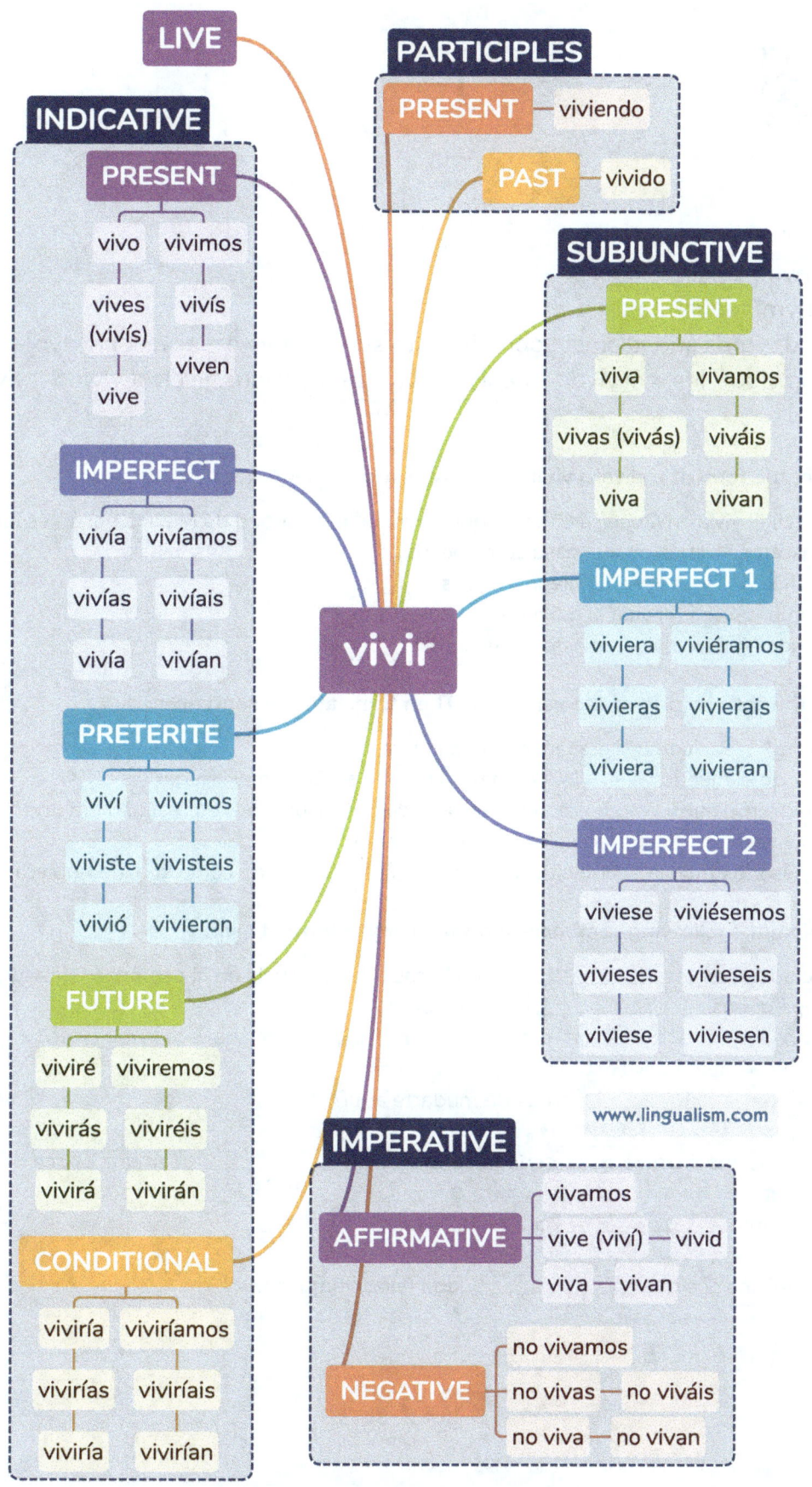

to live
regular -ir verb
- (synonym) existir – to exist
- (antonym) morir – to die
- (related words and idioms) sobrevivir – to survive • vivo – alive • en vivo – (adjective) live • la vida – life • el viver – lifestyle • vivaz – vivacious, lively • vivido – vivid

A. **Identify the form of the verb vivir. Then translate the sentences.**
1. Antes él vivía en Querétaro, hasta que se mudó a la Ciudad de México por su escuela.
2. Nosotros vivimos en una casa cerca del río.
3. Él vivió una vida llena de alegría y risas.
4. Siempre viviré mi vida al máximo.
5. Desde niño he vivido en esta ciudad.

B. **Circle the correct form of the verb vivir. Then translate the sentences.**
1. Vivan/Vievan como si el mañana no existiera.
2. Si todo el mundo vive/viviera en paz, el mundo sería un mejor lugar.
3. Me dijeron que vivían/vivrían en una casa de dos pisos, pero en realidad era una mansión.
4. No vives/vivas del pasado; viva/vive el presente.
5. A pesar de todo lo acontecido, Ariana seguía vivir/viviendo como si nada hubiera pasado.

C. **Complete the following sentences with the correct form of vivir.**
1. De adolescentes _____ en la casa de mi abuela en el campo, a pesar que mi papá quería _____ en la ciudad.
   As teenagers, we lived in my grandmother's house in the country, even though my father wanted to live in the city.
2. ¿Dónde _____ antes de mudarte aquí?
   Where did you live before moving here?
3. A veces imaginamos cómo sería nuestra vida si _____ en una época diferente.
   Sometimes we imagine what our lives would be like if we lived in a different time.
4. Por ahora _____ con mi familia.
   For now I live with my family.
5. La adivina dijo que _____ una feliz y larga vida.
   The fortune teller said you would live a long and happy life.

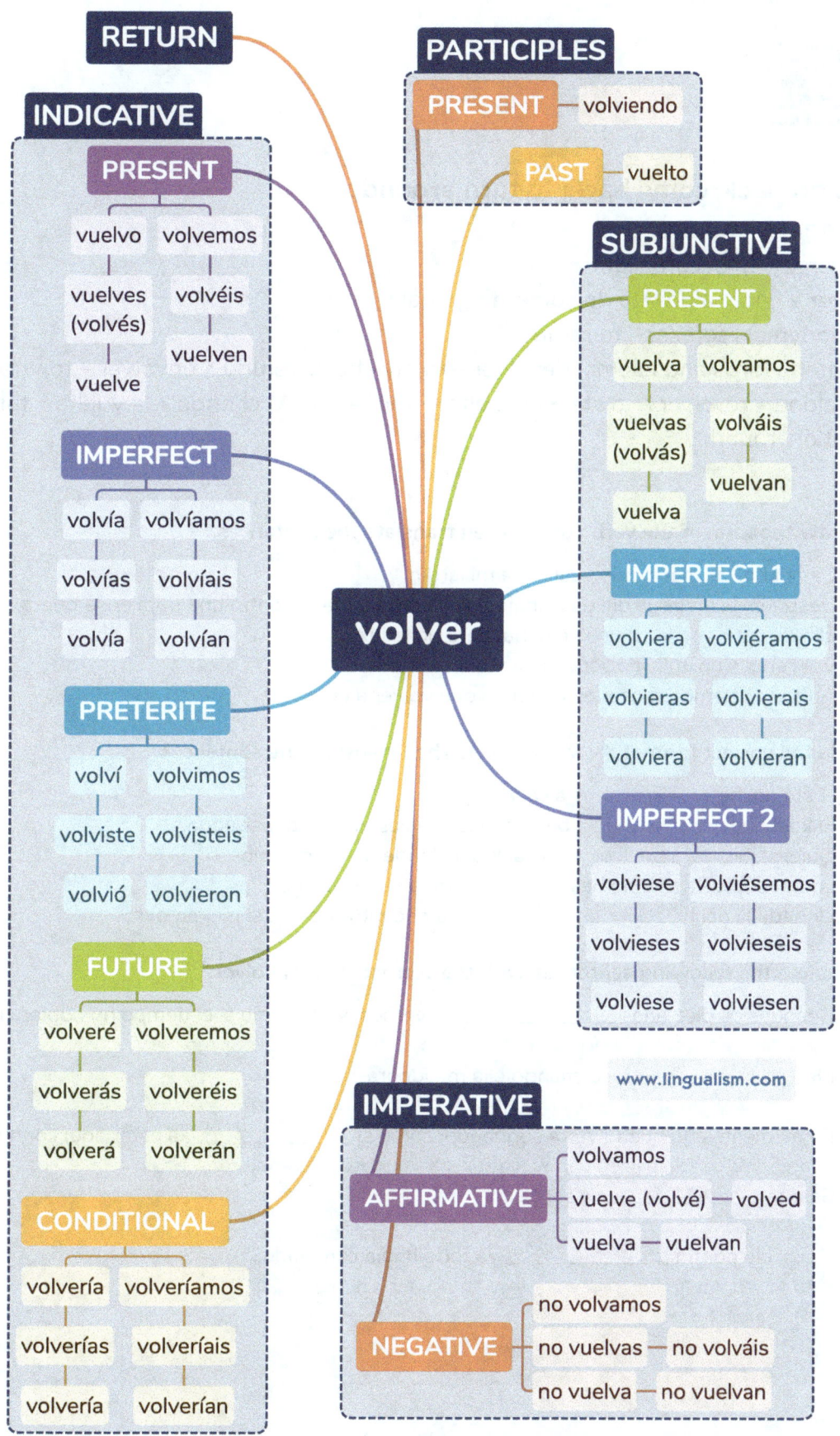

to return, go back, come back; to turn around
stem-changing -er verb: o → ue
- volverse – to become, get
- volver a hacer algo – to do something again
- (synonyms) regresar – to return
- (related words and idioms) devolver – to give back, refund • envolver – to wrap, envelope • revolver – to stir • el vuelto – (money back) change • la vuelta – turn, rotation, round

A. **Identify the form of the verb volver. Then translate the sentences.**
   1. Cada año, las mariposas vuelven a mi jardín.
   2. Después de un largo día de trabajo volví a casa y me encontré una nota en la puerta.
   3. Ella dijo que volvía en una semana, pero no lo hizo.
   4. Volvieras o no, mi vida seguiría siendo la misma.
   5. Aunque estemos cansados tenemos que volver a empezar.

B. **Circle the correct form of the verb volver. Then translate the sentences.**
   1. ¿Esta noche volves/vuelves a casa?
   2. El koala no volvió/vuelvió a bajar de los árboles ni para beber agua.
   3. Quiero que volvamos/volvemos al lugar donde nos conocimos.
   4. Luego del accidente no has vuelto/volvido a ser el mismo.
   5. Llegada la noche volvemos/volveramos a encontrarnos en el mismo bar.

C. **Complete the following sentences with the correct form of volver.**
   1. Después de diez años _____ a vernos, y fue como si el tiempo no hubiera pasado.
      After ten years we met again, and it was as if time had not passed.
   2. Me _____ loco cuando ella me ignora.
      I go crazy when she ignores me.
   3. En mi mente aún puedo verte sonriendo, como si _____ a estar aquí conmigo.
      In my mind I can still see you smiling, as if you were here with me again.
   4. Sé que _____ a ser feliz.
      I know you will be happy again.
   5. Y cuando por fin _____ ya todo había cambiado.
      And when we finally got back, everything had changed.

Answer Key

p. 2 **A.** 1. Yesterday I opened my birthday present and found a new doll. 2. If it wasn't raining, I would open the window. 3. Your cousins opened the restaurant at six in the morning. 4. It is important that you carefully open the old book. 5. Opening the car door, I found a frog on my seat. **B.** 1. *abriste* Did you open the door to let the cats in? 2. *abriera* I doubt she would open the door if she knew what was behind it. 3. *abierto* I have opened the window to let the heat out. 4. *abrió* Luisa opened the bottle of wine and poured a glass for each guest. 5. *abre* She still opens the store every day, even though she has no customers. **C.** 1. *abrirás* 2. *abrirías* 3. *abrió* 4. *abrí* 5. *abrir*

p. 4 **A.** 1. My little brother just learned to read. 2. Let's get this over with! 3. Yesterday the bread ran out, so I'll have to buy more at the supermarket. 4. I need you to finish this project by Monday. 5. My brother is finishing his homework right now. **B.** 1. *acabo* I just finished my favorite book. 2. *acabaste* Did you finish eating all the pizza? 3. *acabado* My son had finished his homework when I got home. 4. *acabó* Did the milk run out? 5. *acabado* I can't believe our vacation is already over. **C.** 1. *acabará* 2. *acabar* 3. *acabado* 4. *acabar* 5. *acaba*

p. 6 **A.** 1. Every day I help my brother with his homework after school. 2. Why aren't you helping your dad fix the car? 3. Juan will help his grandmother run errands tomorrow. 4. Can you help me find my book? 5. It is important that we help others. **B.** 1. *ayudé* I helped my friend change the tire on his car. 2. *ayudaban* Luis and Martha helped their grandmother cook every night. 3. *ayuda* Help your sister! 4. *ayudar* I doubt that she would have been able to help us if she knew what had happened. 5. *ayudábamos* We always helped our neighbors when they needed a hand. **C.** 1. *ayudando* 2. *ayudemos* 3. *ayudado* 4. *ayudarte* 5. *ayudaran*

p. 8 **A.** 1. I was looking for my Spanish book when I realized that I had it in my hand. 2. Alicia was looking for her blouse in my bedroom, but it was in the living room. 3. Juan looked for his favorite book in the library, but it was not there. 4. My mother told me that she would look for my clothes to take them to the laundry. 5. Look for happiness within you and you will find it. **B.** 1. *busqué* I searched all the stores until I found the perfect gift for my sister. 2. *buscamos* We have been looking for a new house to live in for a year. 3. *buscando* Are you looking for someone in particular? 4. *buscas* You seek adventure in everything you do. 5. *buscado* Have you looked for your keys? **C.** 1. *buscar* 2. *buscaron* 3. *buscas* 4. *buscaba* 5. *busques*

p. 10 **A.** 1. I fell off the ladder and hit myself hard. 2. Be careful! Don't fall off the roof! 3. My girlfriend fell from the tree and hurt her leg. 4. When snow falls, everything turns white. 5. She dropped her book on the floor. **B.** 1. *cayó* Last night a branch fell on my car. 2. *caerte* Watch out! You're going to fall if you don't watch where you're stepping. 3. *cayeron* Yesterday tears fell from my eyes when I said goodbye to you. 4. *caía* My dad always told me that if I fell, he would be there to pick me up. 5. *caigas* Don't fall for that scam. **C.** 1. *caer* 2. *cayéndome* 3. *caído* 4. *caí* 5. *caía*

p. 12 **A.** 1. He changed his name to forget his past. 2. I can't change the past, but I can change my future. 3. They changed countries every year because they were very adventurous. 4. I changed my exercise routine to improve my health. 5. We don't want anything to change. **B.** 1. *cambiaron* They changed teams when they knew they weren't going to win. 2. *cambia* Change your son's clothes! He's wet! 3. *cambiaré* I will change jobs next year. 4. *cambies* I want you to change jobs, so you have more time to study. 5. *cambiara, cambió* I wanted my life to change, but nothing changed. **C.** 1. *cambiaría* 2. *cambió* 3. *cambiamos* 4. *cambiar* 5. *cambiemos*

p. 14 **A.** 1. Tomorrow I will start my new diet. 2. Everyone started laughing when I told the joke. 3. I would start my own business if I had more money. 4. Before we started talking, I knew it would be difficult. 5. Unfortunately, I never start my homework on time. **B.** 1. *comenzaras* If you started your day with a cup of coffee, you would feel better. 2. *comienza* The fight begins when the bell rings. 3. *comenzado* I have started running every day to keep fit. 4. *comenzó* It started to rain just as I was going to leave the house.

5. **comiences** Never start running without warming up a bit first. **C.** 1. **comenzó** 2. **comenzado** 3. **comience** 4. **comenzar** 5. **comenzara**

p. 16 A. 1. I have known my best friend for five years. 2. Throughout life, you will meet many interesting people. 3. If you knew the truth, you might not be able to handle it. 4. Yesterday I met a stranger on the bus and now we are friends. 5. In the difficult moments of life is when true friendship is known. **B.** 1. **conocieron** They met when she slipped on the sidewalk and he helped her up. 2. **conocido** I wish I had known the truth before I fell in love with you. 3. **conoce** Do you know the way to the library? 4. **conoces** Sometimes you meet someone, and you know you will be friends forever. 5. **conocía** I didn't know him when I was young, but now he's my best friend. **C.** 1. **conoces** 2. **conozcamos** 3. **conocí** 4. **conocerás** 5. **conocimos**

p. 18 A. 1. You always manage to win in video games. 2. Yesterday we got the tickets for the concert. 3. I had achieved my goal of running a marathon in less than three hours. 4. He always got what he wanted, until they put a stop to it. 5. My dad told me that I have to get a job for the summer. **B.** 1. **conseguir** Roberto always wanted to get a job at the UN, and he finally got it. 2. **conseguido** It has been difficult, but I have managed to overcome my fears. 3. **conseguían** When they were children, they always got the gifts they wanted. 4. **conseguirías** If you worked harder, you would get a better position in the company. 5. **conseguí** I managed to quit smoking thanks to my doctor. **C.** 1. **conseguía** 2. **consiguieras** 3. **conseguiré** 4. **conseguir** 5. **consiguen**

p. 20 A. 1. I can't believe the holidays are over. 2. Do you believe in ghosts? 3. She believed it was impossible, until she succeeded. 4. Don't believe everything you hear. 5. I do not believe in love. **B.** 1. **creyera** It was necessary for him to believe in her. 2. **crea** It is important that she believes in herself. 3. **creer** He couldn't believe that she didn't love him anymore. 4. **creyendo** Believing that he could fly, he jumped from the top of a building. 5. **créame** Believe me! I'm telling you the truth. **C.** 1. **creí** 2. **creyeras** 3. **crees** 4. **creamos** 5. **creería**

p. 22 A. 1. Can I have a piece of your cake? 2. It's better to give than to receive. 3. Don't give me anything! 4. My mom gave me a hug. 5. The doctor will give a lecture tomorrow. **B.** 1. **diste** Did you give the homework to your teacher? 2. **daríamos** If we had more time, we would take a walk around the city. 3. **darte** Tomorrow I'm going to give you an apple for breakfast. 4. **dio** After handing me the package, she turned and left. 5. **damos** We always give our best effort. **C.** 1. **darme** 2. **di** 3. **des** 4. **di** 5. **daban**

p. 24 A. 1. You must study for the exam. 2. We should put aside our egos. 3. I owe a lot of money to my bank. 4. You should help your brother. 5. I should have been more careful, but I tripped and fell. **B.** 1. **deben** Students must always arrive at school on time. 2. **debía** Yesterday Andrés had an exam at seven in the morning and he had to get up early. 3. **deberías** You should try to be less shy around people. 4. **deberás** The following week you will have to look for a new job. 5. **debo** I owe it to my family and my friends. **C.** 1. **debo** 2. **debe** 3. **debía** 4. **deben** 5. **deberíamos**

p. 26 A. 1. Why do you say that? 2. He said that he was tired. 3. When I say I love you, my soul shudders. 4. I won't tell you where the treasure is. 5. Tell the truth to your family. **B.** 1. **dices** If you tell me the truth, I will forgive you. 2. **digan** I trust everyone will say they agree with me. 3. **dijiste** What did you say? I did not understand anything. 4. **dijera** If I told you I love you, would you believe me? 5. **diciendo** I don't like what you're saying. **C.** 1. **dicho** 2. **decíamos** 3. **diré** 4. **digas** 5. **dirían**

p. 28 A. 1. When it started to snow all the children ran outside to play. 2. I always start my day with a cup of coffee. 3. At the end of the movie you started to cry, but I couldn't stop laughing. 4. Do you want me to start cooking dinner? 5. I began to run when it started to rain. **B.** 1. **empezar** It's hard to start over, but I have to. 2. **empezar** I've always wanted to start my own company, and finally I did. 3. **empezando** She was starting to read the book when the earthquake started. 4. **empiece** Always start your day with a smile, and you will see how the rest of the world smiles at you. 5. **empezó** He began playing the guitar after the public asked him to. **C.** 1. **empezamos** 2. **empezó** 3. **empezamos, empezó** 4. **empezaras** 5. **empezaremos**

p. 30 A. 1. After hours of searching the store, I found my favorite book. 2. I have found my lost book. 3. It is important that you find your purpose in life. 4. I always found my cat sleeping in the garden. 5. Seek and you will find, although you will not always find what you are looking for. B. 1. encontraron My children found a gold coin on the way home. 2. encontré I met my friend in the park. 3. encuentra Madrid is located in the middle of Spain. 4. encontrara If Juan found a woman who truly loved him, then he would be happy. 5. encontrado Have you found my keys? C. 1. encontrar 2. encuentra 3. encontrarás 4. encontramos 5. encontré

p. 32 A. 1. Do you understand what I'm trying to say? 2. He didn't understand a word from the board. 3. I just want you to understand me. 4. He understood that he had to work as a team, or else he couldn't win. 5. Everyone got the message. B. 1. entendiste Did you understand what I said? 2. entendió Although no one said anything to him, he understood what he had to do. 3. entiendo I don't understand anything you're saying. 4. entendía He always understood my point of view, even if he didn't agree. 5. entenderé I will never understand people who don't love cats. C. 1. entiendo 2. entendiera 3. entiende 4. entender, entendió 5. entiendes, entenderás

p. 34 A. 1. I wrote a letter to my best friend. 2. I prefer to write by hand than to use the computer. 3. My sister writes poetry in her spare time. 4. I am writing a novel. 5. Every day for two years, I waited for her to write to me. B. 1. escribiría If I had more time, I would write more stories. 2. escribiéndose She was corresponding with a guy she met online, but she blocked him for being rude. 3. escriba It is important that she write down her ideas so that she can remember them. 4. escribe Do you know how to write your name in Chinese? 5. escribir I want to write a letter to my grandmother to tell her everything that has happened this year! C. 1. escribiera 2. escrito 3. escribiré 4. escribo 5. escribas

p. 36 A. 1. When I listen to music, I feel happy. 2. If you listened to what I say, you would have no doubts. 3. Yes, you heard right: I told you to shut up. 4. My little sister always listens to me when I tell her about my problems. 5. They must be quiet so they can hear the sound of the wind through the trees. B. 1. escucha Listen! I never want to see you again. 2. escuchar I couldn't listen to the movie because my brother was making noise. 3. escucharemos For the first time we will hear the concert of our favorite group live. 4. escuchaban My children always listened to their grandmother tell stories of her youth. 5. escuchó At dusk she heard screams coming from the building across the street. C. 1. escuchaba 2. escuchó 3. escucharé 4. escuchar 5. escuchando

p. 38 A. 1. Let's wait for him to come back from vacation to tell him the truth. 2. You will wait for the right time to move house. 3. Two years ago she was expecting a baby. 4. I always wait for my friend after class. 5. I hope your idea works. B. 1. esperaras If you'd wait a bit, we could go together. 2. espera Wait a second, please! 3. esperas Why do you wait for him to call you? 4. esperar I can't wait for the movie to finish to leave. 5. esperas If you wait patiently, everything will work out. C. 1. espero 2. esperaba 3. esperábamos 4. espero 5. esperan

p. 40 A. 1. Do not be sad. Everything will be fine. 2. Why are you sad? 3. I wouldn't be alive if it wasn't for you. 4. I'm not sure in the house where I live. 5. My little brother will be very happy to receive his birthday present. B. 1. estuve I was ill and spent several days in bed. 2. estaba After working all day, I was tired. 3. estar, estás Despite being far away, you are always in my heart. 4. estuviera If I were in the class, I could ask all my doubts to the teacher. 5. está It is raining, and I have no umbrella. C. 1. estaré 2. estaríamos 3. estuviste 4. estamos, estamos 5. esté

p. 42 A. 1. They learned much more by studying with another teacher. 2. Sometimes I study in the library. 3. My sister will study medicine at UNAM. 4. My son studied German in Austria and is now bilingual. 5. If you want to be successful in life, it is important that you study and strive to improve every day. B. 1. estudiara If Susana studied more, she could pass the next exam. 2. estudiábamos Rubí and I were studying in the library when we saw a rat in the hallway. 3. estudia My little brother always studies for his exams. 4. estudié For two years I studied Spanish at university. 5. estudió My dad studied chemical engineering. C. 1. estudiemos 2. estudiarían 3. estudiaste 4. estudie 5. estudiaron

p. 44 A. 1. The last time I played the lottery, I won five dollars. 2. If you keep eating like this you will gain weight. 3. You won the bet, but your friend doesn't seem very happy. 4. In the end, everyone wanted your team to end up winning. 5. Win or lose, enjoy the game. B. 1. **gana** My husband makes more money than me. 2. **ganarán** Do you think they will beat the other school if they cheat? 3. **ganarse** He was trying to make a living as an artist, but it wasn't enough. 4. **ganaste** How much money did you earn last month? 5. **ganado** He is getting better, but he still hasn't won the battle against cancer. C. 1. **ganó** 2. **ganaron** 3. **ganaste, ganando** 4. **ganó** 5. **ganan**

p. 46 A. 1. What fruit do they like? 2. As a child he liked pizza. 3. I would like to dance salsa with you. 4. I don't like people who lie. 5. They like to hang out at the cafe, talking and laughing. B. 1. **gusta** I like coffee. 2. **gusta, gusta** He likes her, and she likes him. 3. **gustó** My girlfriend liked the book I gave her. 4. **gusta** I don't like that you ignore me. 5. **guste** I hope you like the food I prepared. C. 1. **gustaría** 2. **gustarle** 3. **gustó** 4. **gustas** 5. **gusta**

p. 48 A. 1. My godfather has sold his car. 2. In my class, there are more than thirty students. 3. Thanks to your support, you have made a big difference. 4. If we had known, we would not have gone. 5. Once upon a time, there was a princess who lived locked up in a castle. B. 1. **haberte** I'm so glad I saw you! 2. **había** I had always wanted to win a marathon. 3. **había** I had to make a big decision, but thank God I was not wrong. 4. **habrán** They will have finished painting when we arrive. 5. **hubo** Yesterday there was an accident on the way to work. C. 1. **haber** 2. **hayas** 3. **hemos** 4. **habrá** 5. **hubieran, habrían**

p. 50 A. 1. Juan speaks English very well. 2. When they meet, she is going to talk to him about her future. 3. Even though Diviana spoke with a strange accent, everyone understood what she was saying. 4. Although she spoke quietly, it was noticeable that she was angry. 5. When did you last talk to your mother? B. 1. **hables** I recommend that you talk to your mother about what happened. 2. **habla** My mother always speaks to me in Spanish. 3. **hablábamos** When we were dating, we also talked about our differences and how to overcome them. 4. **hablarás** When will you talk to your boss? 5. **habla** She has always loved languages, and she is now fluent in Spanish, French and German. C. 1. **hablo** 2. **hablará** 3. **hablas** 4. **hables, hablar** 5. **habláramos**

p. 52 A. 1. I always do my homework at night. 2. My brother made a cake for my birthday. 3. Can you do me a favor? 4. Last month we made a surprise trip to Mexico. 5. Let's make a deal: if you help me with my homework, I'll buy you a pizza. B. 1. **haces** Hello Paula! What are you doing? 2. **hacía** It was very hot, and I needed a cold drink. 3. **hagas** I don't want you to get your hopes up because something can go wrong. 4. **hiciera** I didn't think it would be that hot. 5. **hagamos** Let's not do anything tonight. C. 1. **hice** 2. **hacían** 3. **haré** 4. **haga** 5. **hizo**

p. 54 A. 1. Every day I go to my work by bus. 2. I'd rather you go to the party with her. 3. Everything will be fine. 4. Yesterday they went to the beach and saw a dolphin. 5. Where would you go if you had a time machine? B. 1. **iba** I met your uncle when he was on his way to your house. 2. **irás** If you continue committing crimes you will go to jail. 3. **fuera** He always looked at her like he was going to tell her something, but he never did. 4. **fue** Where did you go? 5. **van** They go to the beach. C. 1. **vas** 2. **fui** 3. **vamos** 4. **íbamos** 5. **fuiste**

p. 56 A. 1. I want to play soccer, but I don't have a team. 2. My friends and I play soccer every weekend. 3. Every day we play video games at home. 4. When you play cards with your family, you always win. 5. My brother and I are playing baseball. B. 1. **jugaban** Every day after school the children played chess in the park. 2. **juega** My cat always plays with the tennis ball. 3. **jueguen** It is important for children to play. 4. **juego** I always play the lottery with my uncles. 5. **jugaron** Last night the boys played basketball in the park until dark. C. 1. **jugué** 2. **jugara** 3. **jugar** 4. **jugarás** 5. **juegan**

p. 58 A. 1. Have you read that book yet? 2. My brother reads a lot. 3. I usually read a lot of horror stories, even if I can't sleep afterwards. 4. Several years ago I had read that book; I no longer remembered. 5. When he was a child, he read every day. B. 1. **leas** After you read this book, you will see the world differently. 2. **léeme** Please read me a story. 3. **leyeron** They both read all three books in one month. 4. **leyendo** I was reading a horror book when I heard a noise. 5. **leí** After years without hearing from him, today I read an email from my friend. C. 1. **lee** 2. **leerá** 3. **leerías** 4. **leemos** 5. **leyera**

p. 60 A. 1. When María arrived at the party, she knew it would be an unforgettable night. 2. Juan Gabriel never imagined that he would become so famous. 3. You arrived just in time. 4. The time will come when you realize what really matters. 5. I hope my taxi arrives soon. B. 1. **llegué** I arrived at the airport and realized that I had forgotten my passport. 2. **llegaron** Tourists came to the city and were amazed at its beauty. 3. **llegabas** You were always late for work and your boss had to scold you. 4. **llego** When I get home, I start to watch TV. 5. **llegarás** You won't be on time! C. 1. **lleguemos** 2. **llegarían** 3. **llegó** 4. **llegaste, llegué** 5. **llegaras**

p. 62 A. 1. Look mom, a rainbow! 2. She was looking out the window when she noticed that it had started to rain. 3. Axel always looked out the window when he had to do something he didn't want to. 4. If you look carefully at the map, how many buildings do you recognize? 5. After she looked at her haggard appearance in the mirror, she knew that she needed to change her eating habits. B. 1. **miró** Raquel looked up at the sky and it was full of bright stars. 2. **mires** I haven't asked you for anything yet, except that you look me in the face and don't run away. 3. **mira** When people look at me, I feel like they're judging me. 4. **mirando** Karen was looking out the window when someone she knew walked by. 5. **miraba** He was staring at her, but she was ignoring him. C. 1. **miré** 2. **mirar** 3. **mira** 4. **miró** 5. **mirar, mirar**

p. 64 A. 1. If I die, I want you to know that I loved you. 2. I felt like I was dying of thirst, but the water was contaminated. 3. Never give up without a fight, or you will die regretful. 4. They all died in a car accident. 5. Every year thousands of people die of hunger around the world. B. 1. **morir** My aunt is very ill, and we all know that she is going to die soon. 2. **muera** I don't want anyone else to die. 3. **mueren** How many people die each month in the world because of tobacco? 4. **murió** Two days after burying his wife, he too died. 5. **muriera** Before Doña Gregoria died, she made one last wish. C. 1. **moriría** 2. **murió** 3. **morir** 4. **mueras** 5. **morimos**

p. 66 A. 1. I need a new computer. 2. Do you need my help? 3. My family needed a place to live. 4. I was so sick that I needed help to finish the project. 5. We need world leaders to take action to protect our planet. B. 1. **necesitan** All people need money to meet their needs. 2. **necesitábamos** When we lived in the desert, we constantly needed new provisions. 3. **necesitas** With the birth of your child, you need to find a new job. 4. **necesito** I don't need more than what I already have. 5. **necesitan** Currently students need to study a lot to pass the exam. C. 1. **necesitarán** 2. **necesita** 3. **necesitarán** 4. **necesito** 5. **necesites**

p. 68 A. 1. I can't pay the rent this month. 2. Unless they pay me, I won't do it. 3. Did you pay the phone bill? 4. On my vacations, I always paid in cash, never by card. 5. She would pay to go to the moon. B. 1. **pagues** I don't want you to pay for my food. 2. **pago** I always pay my cards on time. 3. **pagué** Yesterday I paid my neighbor ten dollars to wash my car. 4. **pagado** I have already paid my internet bill! 5. **pague** Please pay the bill before you leave. C. 1. **pagarás** 2. **pagara** 3. **pagamos** 4. **pagaré** 5. **pagan**

p. 70 A. 1. My relatives thought it was a good day for a walk, but the rain ruined it. 2. I could not stop thinking about her. 3. I always think of you. 4. I never thought it would be so hard to quit smoking. 5. What are you planning to do tomorrow? B. 1. **pensara** It is likely that he only thought of himself. 2. **pienses** It is important that you think about what you want to do in life. 3. **pienso** I think you're going to be a great father. 4. **pensé** I thought I'd never see you again. 5. **piensas** Why don't you think about the consequences? C. 1. **pensar** 2. **pensando** 3. **pensamos** 4. **pienso** 5. **pensaré**

p. 72 A. 1. No matter how hard it is, I know I can do it. 2. If I could, I would like to be invisible. 3. We could always count on each other. 4. Rebeca couldn't help but cry when she saw him. 5. Roberto was afraid that his parents would never accept him. B. 1. **podía** She could hear the joy in his voice. 2. **podríamos** We could have been friends, but it's too late. 3. **puede** She may not be perfect, but she is my mother and I love her. 4. **podrás** Next time you can do better. 5. **pueda** Let her walk as far as she can. C. 1. **pude** 2. **podrías** 3. **pudiste** 4. **puede** 5. **podido**

p. 74 **A.** 1. I usually set my alarm to wake me up at six in the morning, but yesterday I forgot. 2. My students get nervous when they have to speak in public. 3. Put the cake in the oven. 4. She put on the new dress I bought her. 5. Have you set the table for dinner yet? **B.** 1. ponía Before the pandemic, I would set my alarm to wake me up at seven. 2. ponía Sometimes he would meditate as if reconsidering what he was going to say. 3. pondrá He will first put the food in the oven, and then he will call his family to have dinner together. 4. pusimos We put the books in the box. 5. pones When you put your chest next to mine, the world stops. **C.** 1. pongamos 2. puso 3. pone 4. pongas 5. pusieras

p. 76 **A.** 1. María asked Pedro if he wanted to have dinner with her that night. 2. Can I ask you a question? 3. Whenever they are sick, children ask about their toys. 4. I always wonder what my life would be like if I had made a different decision. 5. I don't like people asking me my age. **B.** 1. pregunté I asked my sister if she would lend me her car, but she said no. 2. preguntaba She was asking me if you could come to my house and bless her. 3. preguntas Why do you ask so many things? 4. preguntó He asked if he could go to the bathroom before class started. 5. preguntado I have asked ten people and none of them knew the answer. **C.** 1. preguntó 2. preguntaste 3. preguntes 4. preguntaron 5. pregunta

p. 78 **A.** 1. My grandmother wants me to visit her tomorrow. 2. I want my boyfriend to buy me a diamond ring. 3. We will love each other even if we are far away. 4. I wanted to be happy, but happiness is a state of mind. 5. Do what you want! **B.** 1. quiero I love you, but I can't be with you. 2. quería I wanted to be a writer, but acting caught my attention more. 3. quise I always wanted to be a successful person, and now I am. 4. queramos Even if we don't want to, we have to finish the report today. 5. quieres Do you want to go to the movies with me tonight? **C.** 1. querrás 2. quisiste 3. quisieras 4. quiero 5. quisieron

p. 80 **A.** 1. I received a perfect grade on my Spanish test! 2. When you receive a package in the mail, do you take long to pick it up? 3. Students are given many opportunities to pass the semester. 4. Do you think we'll get our packages in time for the party? 5. I was getting a pizza when I heard a sound behind the door. **B.** 1. recibió My boss received a mysterious package at the office. 2. recibido We have received a gift from our grandparents. 3. recibes What do you do when you receive a rejection letter from the university? 4. recibiéramos I'm glad we finally got the news. 5. recibe Many people receive help from the government each year. **C.** 1. recibieron 2. reciba 3. recibiría 4. recibimos 5. recibía

p. 82 **A.** 1. From a young age I knew that she wanted to be a doctor. 2. I don't know if it's going to rain soon. 3. He always looked at her in a special way, as if he knew what she was thinking. 4. I will never know if what she told me was true or a lie. 5. Why didn't you let me know? **B.** 1. sabe She knows that she has to study but she prefers to play video games. 2. supiste How did you know it was me? 3. sabrías If you had studied astronomy, you would know that. 4. supieran I don't think they knew the truth. 5. sabido You have known how to overcome this ferocious and brutal disease. **C.** 1. supiste 2. sabe 3. supimos 4. sabremos 5. sepa

p. 84 **A.** 1. On Saturday I left work and went straight home. 2. When we lived in Madrid, we went out every day to buy bread. 3. She was getting out of the shower when she heard a noise and freaked out. 4. He always hangs out with his friends. 5. Every morning I leave the house to go to work. **B.** 1. salgan Get out of my house right now! 2. salía Whenever I got out of school, I would go to the candy store. 3. salí As soon as I left home, I realized that I forgot my cell phone. 4. salieras If you left earlier, we could spend more time together. 5. saldrían If it were not cloudy, they would go out to see the eclipse. **C.** 1. salió 2. salga 3. saldremos 4. salen 5. saliéramos

p. 86 **A.** 1. Cats are very intelligent animals. 2. Enrique was a very rich man, but he was not happy. 3. What are the dogs looking for? 4. It would be a dream come true if I could win the lottery. 5. If it wasn't for my family, I don't know where I would be today. **B.** 1. seremos We will not be students all the time. 2. es It is impossible to ignore the fact that she is beautiful. 3. sea It is a shame he's so dumb. 4. soy I am a very organized person. 5. seas Do not be rude! **C.** 1. somos, somos 2. sido 3. éramos 4. fuiste 5. eres

p. 88 **A.** 1. Until yesterday I had a secret, but now the whole world knows it. 2. I hope she is never afraid to be different. 3. I have an idea how we can escape. 4. Be careful with the fire! 5. You had a very poor childhood, but you never stopped fighting for your dreams. **B. 1. tenemos** It's quaking/shaking and we have to get out right now. **2. tuviste** You had a very difficult life, but you always got up. **3. tuviera** If I had a time machine, I would travel back to the time of the dinosaurs. **4. tuvo** After the hurricane he had to leave his home. **5. tenían** My grandparents had a big house in the city. **C. 1. tienes 2. tendré 3. tengamos 4. tenemos 5. tenido**

p. 90 A. 1. She drinks a cup of coffee every morning. 2. Marcos got up late and now he will take a taxi to get to work. 3. She took his hand and said, "I love you." 4. Come in and grab a book from the shelf. 5. They needed to make a quick decision. **B. 1. tomé** After much thought, I finally made the decision to leave the country. **2. tomaste** Why did you make the decision not to go to college? **3. tomabas** Did you say you were on/taking sleep meds? **4. tomarían** I thought the kids would take my money, but I was wrong. **5. tomo** When I finish work, I have my cup of coffee and sit down to watch the sunset. **C. 1. tomaremos 2. tomaron 3. tomaríamos 4. tomar 5. tomando**

p. 92 A. 1. He works in an office, and she in a factory. 2. Ever since I can remember, I have always been working as a teacher. 3. I always work hard to get what I want. 4. I know you worked in a factory, but the factory closed, and you can't go back to it anymore. 5. Although her father insisted that she work, she wanted to study. **B. 1. trabajamos** Yesterday we worked until ten at night. **2. trabajarías** You never imagined that you would work as a waitress, but here you are. **3. trabajemos** We need (us) to work together to finish this project. **4. trabajado** I have worked a lot this week. **5. trabajó** She always worked hard, even when no one was looking at her. **C. 1. trabajábamos 2. trabajarán 3. trabajaba 4. trabajar 5. trabajaras**

p. 94 A. 1. Why did you tell me that you were coming if you didn't plan to do it? 2. I came here to look for work. 3. Are you coming to my house tonight? 4. Come to my house and I will give you a surprise. 5. You came from far away to see this beautiful landscape. **B. 1. venga** I can't believe my dad isn't coming to my graduation. **2. vino** The boy came to ask his mother for a cookie. **3. viene** My mother comes from Mexico. **4. vendríamos** If we could, we would come to see you every day. **5. ven** Come, I need you. **C. 1. vendré 2. vienen 3. vendría 4. vengamos 5. vinieran**

p. 96 A. 1. Without my glasses, I can't see anything. 2. Tonight you will see the full moon. 3. I know you won't believe me, but yesterday I saw a UFO. 4. I have never seen so many stars in the sky. 5. See that red car? It's mine! **B. 1. vieron** María and José saw each other at the supermarket and did not greet each other. **2. vio** Alejandra saw her brother on the street with a woman she didn't recognize. **3. viera** She looked around her to make sure no one saw her, then she stole the jewel. **4. veían** Through the window, the children saw the approaching storm. **5. ve** My little sister always watches movies before me. **C. 1. vimos 2. vería 3. veremos 4. veo 5. verlo**

p. 98 A. 1. Before, he lived in Querétaro, until he moved to Mexico City for his school. 2. We live in a house near the river. 3. He lived a life full of joy and laughter. 4. I will always live my life to the fullest. 5. I have lived in this city since I was a child. **B. 1. vivan** Live as if tomorrow does not exist. **2. viviera** If everyone lived in peace, the world would be a better place. **3. vivían** They told me they lived in a two-story house, but it was actually a mansion. **4. vivas, vive** Don't live in the past; live in the present. **5. viviendo** Despite everything that had happened, Ariana continued to live as if nothing had happened. **C. 1. vivíamos, vivir 2. viviste 3. viviéramos 4. vivo 5. vivirías**

p. 100 A. 1. Every year the butterflies return to my garden. 2. After a long day at work I came home to find a note on my door. 3. She said she'd be back in a week, but she didn't do it. 4. Whether you came back or not, my life would still be the same. 5. Even though we're tired, we have to start over. **B. 1. vuelves** Are you coming home tonight? **2. volvió** The koala did not come down from the trees again, not even to drink water. **3. volvamos** I want us to go back to the place where we met. **4. vuelto** After the accident, you have not been the same again. **5. volvemos** At night we meet again in the same bar. **C. 1. volvimos 2. vuelvo 3. volvieras 4. volverás 5. volvimos**

www.ingramcontent.com/pod-product-compliance
Lightning Source LLC
Chambersburg PA
CBHW051806100526
44592CB00016B/2590